Measurement: Grade 5

Table of Contents

Measurement: Grade 5

Introduction

Teachers are well aware of the importance of developing strong mathematics skills in their students. Students, on the other hand, may not understand how math will be a useful tool outside of school. That is why application of math skills, once mastered, to real-life situations is vital to students' appreciation of math.

Mathematics skills are used in almost every aspect of our lives, from an early age. Students may not realize that they are using math skills when they build, draw, cook, or score a game. By showing them that these skills do relate to math, teachers and parents can help students make the connection.

Measurement is one of the most common ways that students will use mathematics, both as students and as adults. From dressing for the weather to coming home on time or spending allowances, students estimate and use measurement skills throughout their day.

The National Council for Teachers of Mathematics (NCTM) has set standards for mathematical content and the processes through which students should gain and use their knowledge. Measurement is one of the five content areas set forth in the standards. In the fifth grade, students should use a variety of tools and techniques to measure, apply the results in problem-solving situations, and communicate the reasoning used in solving these problems. This book provides opportunities for learning measurement concepts in accordance with the NCTM standards.

Organization

Measurement is divided into eight units covering estimation, length, capacity, temperature, mass, time, money, and computation. Each unit provides opportunities for hands-on learning as well as applications to real-life situations. Students use estimation skills and then prove their measurements. Part of each unit is devoted to metric measurements. Tools needed for hands-on activities are listed at the bottom of the page.

Each unit in *Measurement* is preceded by an assessment for that unit. There is also an overall assessment that covers all of the measurement skills in the book. Each of the tests can be used as a pretest to gauge students' areas of strength or weakness, as well as a posttest to demonstrate what students have learned. The overall test can be used as a pretest to give the teacher a clearer picture of the units in which students need the most practice. It can also be used as a posttest to demonstrate improvement or highlight areas that still require attention.

Use

Measurement is designed to complement existing math programs. It is intended for independent use by students who have had instruction in the specific skills covered in the lessons. Copies of the activity sheets can be given to individuals, pairs of students, or groups of students for completion. When students are familiar with the content of the worksheets, they can be assigned as homework.

Determine the implementation that best fits your students' needs and your classroom structure. The following plan suggests a format for implementation.

1. Administer the overall assessment to establish baseline information on each student. You may choose to concentrate on certain units after reviewing the test results. Administer unit assessments before

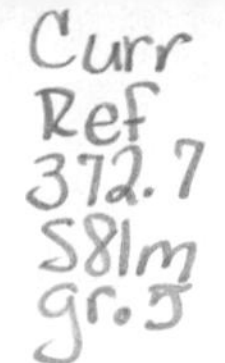

Measurement: Grade 5

Introduction (continued)

beginning a unit. When the unit is finished, you may use the unit assessments as posttests. The overall assessment may also be administered after a student, group of students, or the entire class has completed the book. Explain the purpose of the assessment tests to the class.

2. Explain the purpose of the worksheets to the class.

3. Review the mechanics of how you would like students to work with the activities. Will they work in pairs? Are the activities for homework?

4. Introduce the students to the process and purpose of the activities. Work with students when they have difficulty. Assign only a few pages at a time to avoid pressure.

Additional Notes

Parent Communication—Send the Letter to Parents home with students.

Student Communication—Read the Letter to Students to the class. Answer any questions that arise. Encourage students to share the letter with their parents.

Bulletin Board—Display completed worksheets or projects to show student progress.

Student Progress Chart—Duplicate the grid sheets found on pages 6–7. Record student names in the left column. Note date of completion of each lesson for each student. If students are working independently according to individual areas of weakness, you may wish to highlight the units in which students need practice for convenient reference.

Curriculum Correlation—This chart helps you with cross-curriculum lesson planning.

Have Fun!—Working with these activities should be fun as well as meaningful for you and your students.

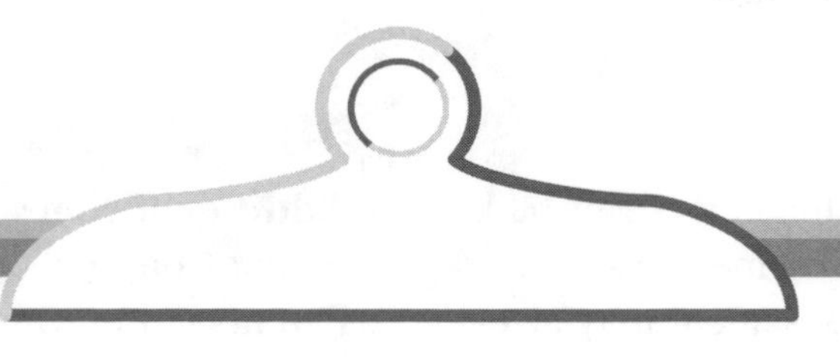

Dear Parent,

During this school year, our class will be working with measurement skills. We will be completing activity sheets that will strengthen skills in measurement. We will use estimation and measure length, capacity, temperature, and mass. We will study time and money and do computations in measurement.

From time to time, I may send home activity sheets. To best help your child, please consider the following suggestions:

- Provide a quiet place to work.
- Go over the directions on the worksheet together. See that your child understands what is being asked.
- Encourage your child to do his or her best.
- Check the lesson when it is complete.
- Go over your child's work, and note improvements as well as problems.

Help your child maintain a positive attitude about mathematics. Let your child know that each lesson provides an opportunity to have fun and to learn. If your child expresses anxiety about the work, talk to your child about ways to eliminate these feelings. Your relaxed attitude and support will help to reduce your child's anxiety.

Enjoy this time that you spend with your child. With your help, his or her skills will improve with each activity completed.

Thank you for your support!

Cordially,

Dear Student,

An important part of what we do this year in math will be working with measurement. You may not even think about it, but you use measurement many times each day. You use measurement when you check the weather, look at the time, or buy your lunch. Measurement is math!

The activities in the measurement book we use will be fun. You will see how learning about measurement can be very useful to you! You may be cooking, guessing the number of jellybeans in a jar, or moving the furniture around in your room. All of these things use your skills in measurement.

When you complete a worksheet, remember to:

- Read the directions carefully. What are you being asked to do?
- Read each question carefully. All the questions on a page may not be the same.
- Check your answers when you are finished.

Have fun as you measure your way through math!

Sincerely,

Measurement: Grade 5

Student Progress Chart

STUDENT NAME	UNIT 1 ESTIMATION										UNIT 2 LENGTH										UNIT 3 CAPACITY										UNIT 4 TEMPERATURE									
	13	14	15	16	17	18	19	20	21	22	23	24	25	26	27	28	29	30	31	32	33	34	35	36	37	38	39	40	41	42	43	44	45	46	47	48	49	50	51	52

Measurement: Grade 5

Student Progress Chart, p. 2

STUDENT NAME	UNIT 5 MASS								UNIT 6 TIME										UNIT 7 MONEY										UNIT 8 COMPUTATION													
	53	54	55	56	57	58	59	60	61	62	63	64	65	66	67	68	69	70	71	72	73	74	75	76	77	78	79	80	81	82	83	84	85	86	87	88	89	90	91	92	93	94

Measurement: Grade 5

Curriculum Correlation

	Social Studies	Physical Education	Science	Art	Language Arts
Unit 1: Estimation		15	18		15, 16, 17, 18, 19, 20, 21, 22
Unit 2: Length	29, 30, 32				25, 26, 29, 30, 31, 32
Unit 3: Capacity		42			39, 40, 41, 42
Unit 4: Temperature	52		45, 46, 47, 48, 49, 50, 51, 52	52	48, 49, 50, 51, 52
Unit 5: Mass					58, 59, 60
Unit 6: Time	67			70	63, 65, 66, 67, 68, 69, 70
Unit 7: Money	75	79		80	74, 75, 76, 77, 78, 79, 80
Unit 8: Computation		93		92, 93, 94	88, 91, 92, 93, 94

Name ______________________ Date ______________

Overall Assessment

Measurement: Grade 5

DIRECTIONS

Read each question. Darken the circle by the correct answer.

Unit 1: Estimation

1. What would be the best unit to use to measure the length of a road?

Ⓐ inches
Ⓑ feet
Ⓒ miles

2. What would be the best unit to use to measure the amount of liquid in a contact lens case?

Ⓐ milliliters
Ⓑ kiloliters
Ⓒ liters

3. Mr. Bing teaches art to all the students in grades K through 8. There are 653 students in all. Mr. Bing's classes hold an average of 23 students each. If the students each have 1 art class every week, about how many classes does Mr. Bing teach each week?

Ⓐ about 30
Ⓑ about 20
Ⓒ about 40

4. Gordon bought 2 lacrosse balls for $3.15 each, a stick for $35.99, and gloves for $27.05. About how much did Gordon spend in all?

Ⓐ about $70
Ⓑ about $50
Ⓒ about $66

Unit 2: Length

5. Which of these would best be measured using centimeters?

Ⓐ a pen
Ⓑ a motorcycle
Ⓒ a bed

6. Mt. Fuji is 3,776 meters high, Mt. Etna is 3,390 meters high, and Mt. Cook is 3,764 meters high. What is the difference between the highest and the lowest peaks?

Ⓐ 12 meters
Ⓑ 386 meters
Ⓒ 368 meters

7. Luigi needs 8 yards of wood for some shelves. The lumber is sold by the foot. How many feet of lumber will Luigi need to buy?

Ⓐ 8 feet
Ⓑ 16 feet
Ⓒ 24 feet

8. James' stilts are 6 feet tall. Daniel's stilts are 2 yards tall. Whose stilts are taller?

Ⓐ James' stilts
Ⓑ Daniel's stilts
Ⓒ They are the same height.

Go on to the next page.

Name ______________________ Date ____________

Overall Assessment

Measurement: Grade 5, p. 2

DIRECTIONS

Read each question. Darken the circle by the correct answer.

Unit 3: Capacity

9. Which would be the best unit to measure the amount of water used during a shower?

Ⓐ cups
Ⓑ gallons
Ⓒ quarts

10. Connor picked 16 quarts of berries on Tuesday and 12 quarts on Thursday. How many pints of berries did he pick altogether?

Ⓐ 56
Ⓑ 32
Ⓒ 28

11. Gillian has 800 mL of juice in a jar. How much more juice does she need to fill a 2-L container?

Ⓐ 200 mL
Ⓑ 120 mL
Ⓒ 1,200 mL

12. Harry needs 2 cups of sugar to make a double batch of brownies. He has 6 cups of sugar. How many single batches of brownies could he make?

Ⓐ 4 batches
Ⓑ 6 batches
Ⓒ 3 batches

Unit 4: Temperature

13. Which is the best estimate of the temperature on a good day to go ice skating at the neighborhood rink?

Ⓐ 45° F
Ⓑ 62° F
Ⓒ 30° F

14. When Tia woke up, her thermometer read 12° C. By the afternoon, it was freezing. By how many degrees had the temperature dropped?

Ⓐ 12
Ⓑ 10
Ⓒ 13

15. The Smith family reunion is at the beach. Everyone has worked up a huge appetite swimming in the ocean. Which of these is the most likely temperature of the air?

Ⓐ 63° F
Ⓑ 84° F
Ⓒ 59° F

16. A pot of water has just begun to boil. What is the best estimate of the temperature of the water?

Ⓐ 185° F
Ⓑ 360° F
Ⓒ 212° F

Go on to the next page.

Name ____________________ Date ____________

Overall Assessment

Measurement: Grade 5, p. 3

DIRECTIONS

Read each question. Darken the circle by the correct answer.

Unit 5: Mass

17. Mr. Reyna filled 9 seed bags equally with 81 pounds of thistle seed. How many ounces of thistle seed fit into each bag?

Ⓐ 144 ounces
Ⓑ 9 ounces
Ⓒ 72 ounces

18. Don's truck can carry 1 ton. He has items that weigh 400 pounds, 350 pounds, and 175 pounds. How much more weight can he carry?

Ⓐ 925 pounds
Ⓑ 1,075 pounds
Ⓒ 75 pounds

19. Which unit of measure would be best to use to find the weight of a speedboat?

Ⓐ grams
Ⓑ milligrams
Ⓒ kilograms

20. What is the best estimate of the weight of a box of cereal?

Ⓐ 600 mg
Ⓑ 600 g
Ⓒ 600 kg

Unit 6: Time

21. Lupe walked her dog 20 minutes a day for 9 weeks. How many hours did Lupe walk the dog?

Ⓐ 21 hours
Ⓑ 8 hours
Ⓒ 180 hours

22. Tim's school day begins at 7:40 A.M. and ends at 2:10 P.M. He spends an average of 1 hour and 45 minutes on homework each night. How much of Tim's day is taken up by school and homework?

Ⓐ 7 hours and 20 minutes
Ⓑ 8 hours and 15 minutes
Ⓒ 9 hours and 5 minutes

23. It takes Carl 12 minutes to walk around a track. He can run around the track twice as fast as he can walk. How long would it take Carl to run around the track 7 times?

Ⓐ 42 minutes
Ⓑ 84 minutes
Ⓒ 21 minutes

24. It takes Jackie 12 seconds to run to the end of her driveway. How many times can Jackie run the length of her driveway and back in 5 minutes?

Ⓐ $15\frac{1}{2}$ times
Ⓑ 25 times
Ⓒ $12\frac{1}{2}$ times

Go on to the next page.

Name ______________________ Date ______________

Overall Assessment

Measurement: Grade 5, p. 4

DIRECTIONS

Read each question. Darken the circle by the correct answer.

Unit 7: Money

25. Keisha bought a package of baseball cards for $1.50, a pen for $3.99, and nail polish for $1.75. If she paid $0.50 tax, about how much did Keisha spend altogether?

Ⓐ about $11
Ⓑ about $8
Ⓒ about $5

26. Joel bought 2 computer games that cost $29.99 each and a new joystick for $19.99. If Joel gave the cashier 4 $20 bills, how much change did he receive?

Ⓐ $0.03
Ⓑ $1.03
Ⓒ $30.02

27. Stan has $6.00 in his wallet and $1.32 in change in his pocket. Which combination of coins and bills could he have?

Ⓐ 6 $1 bills, 3 quarters, and 6 pennies
Ⓑ A $5 bill, a $1 bill, 3 quarters, 5 dimes, 1 nickel, and 2 pennies
Ⓒ A $5 bill, a $1 bill, 2 quarters, 6 nickels, and 1 penny

Unit 8: Computation

28. What is the perimeter of a square that is 3 yd on each side?

Ⓐ 6 yd
Ⓑ 12 yd
Ⓒ 9 yd

29. What is the circumference of a circle, rounded to the nearest tenth, with a diameter of 23 in.?

Ⓐ 72.2 in.
Ⓑ 68.4 in.
Ⓒ 72.6 in.

30. A pool is 9 meters deep, 10 meters wide, and 13 meters long. What is the volume of the pool?

Ⓐ 1,170 cubic meters
Ⓑ 560 cubic meters
Ⓒ 2,850 cubic meters

31. Bo's room is 9 feet long by 12 feet wide. His closet floor is 3 feet deep by 6 feet wide. How many square feet of carpet does he need to cover the entire area?

Ⓐ 126 ft^2
Ⓑ 108 ft^2
Ⓒ 144 ft^2

Name ______________________ Date ____________

Unit 1 Assessment

Estimation

DIRECTIONS

Read each problem and solve. Darken the circle by the correct answer.

1. What unit of measure would be best to determine the length of a football field?

Ⓐ meters
Ⓑ centimeters
Ⓒ kilometers

2. Which unit of measure is best to use to describe the weight of a candle?

Ⓐ tons
Ⓑ pounds
Ⓒ ounces

3. Which of these has a weight that is best measured in grams?

Ⓐ an apple
Ⓑ a couch
Ⓒ a girl

4. Elsa went to bed at 8:45 P.M. She woke up at 6:30 A.M. About how many hours did Elsa sleep?

Ⓐ about 10 hours
Ⓑ about 12 hours
Ⓒ about 11 hours

5. The temperature outside was a little too cold for swimming, so the children collected shells on the beach instead. The temperature was most likely

Ⓐ 67° F.
Ⓑ 30° F.
Ⓒ 81° F.

6. Julia uses $\frac{1}{2}$ cup of applesauce for each loaf of bread she makes. On Friday, she had enough orders to use $7\frac{1}{2}$ quarts of applesauce. About how many loaves of bread had been ordered?

Ⓐ about 55
Ⓑ about 40
Ⓒ about 60

Go on to the next page.

Name ______________________ Date ____________

Unit 1 Assessment

Estimation, p. 2

DIRECTIONS

Read each problem and solve. Darken the circle by the correct answer.

7. Sandy has $25.00. She wants to buy 2 shirts and a pair of pants at the Bargain Barn. The shirts cost $7.99 each, and the pants are $13.25. About how much more money does she need to buy all 3 items?

Ⓐ about $1.00
Ⓑ about $4.00
Ⓒ about $3.00

8. Faoud went shopping for his mother. He bought butter for $1.95, oranges for $2.17, and crackers for $1.89. He gave the cashier $10.00. About how much money did he get back?

Ⓐ about $6.00
Ⓑ about $4.00
Ⓒ about $3.00

9. Julius and his mother bought hamburger for a family cookout. About how much did they probably buy?

Ⓐ 80 lb
Ⓑ 800 lb
Ⓒ 8 lb

10. Which unit of measure would you use to describe the weight of a bushel of apples?

Ⓐ kilogram
Ⓑ centimeter
Ⓒ liter

11. A rectangle is $5\frac{3}{4}$ inches on one side and $2\frac{1}{4}$ inches on the other side. Estimate the perimeter.

Ⓐ about 13 inches
Ⓑ about 16 inches
Ⓒ about 8 inches

12. To set up a science experiment, Kent must first fill each of 4 test tubes with 2.5 milliliters of hydrogen peroxide. About how much hydrogen peroxide does Kent need to fill all 4 tubes?

Ⓐ about 100 mL
Ⓑ about 8 mL
Ⓒ about 12 mL

Name ______________________________ Date ______________

Just Jump!

DIRECTIONS

You are going to make a double-line graph that shows how closely your class can estimate how high they can jump. Each student should estimate how high he or she can jump from a standing position, and share that information with the rest of the class for their graph. Then, each student will jump, one at a time, while another student marks the height of the jump. (If there is a student in your class who cannot jump, he or she should be the official height measurer.)

Write the students' names or initials along the bottom of the graph. Mark a red point for each student's estimate. Then draw a red line from each point to the next, starting at the left of the graph. Then mark a point, in blue, for each student's actual jumping height. Draw a blue line through these points. How close are your lines to being the same?

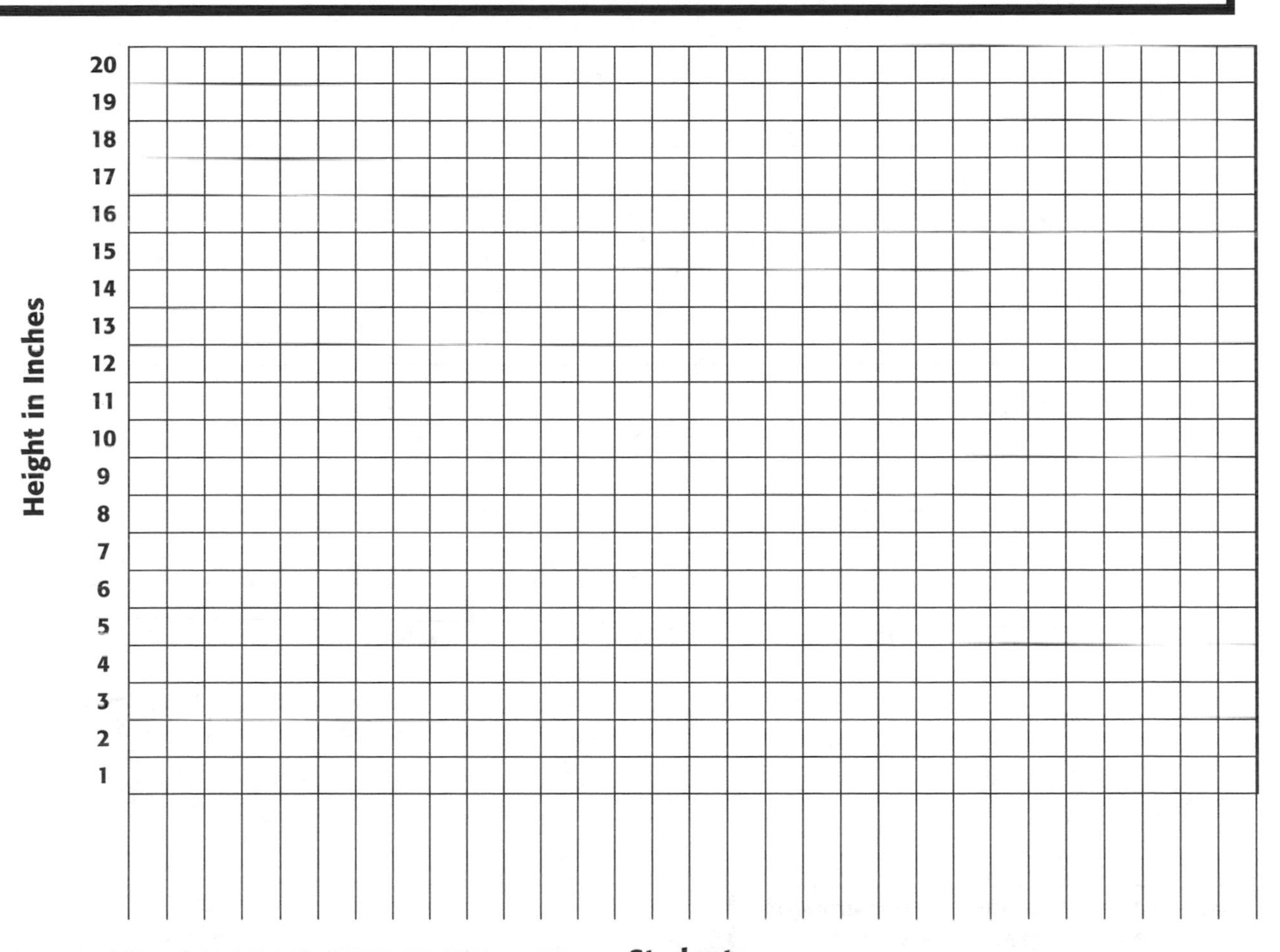

Tools: red and blue pencils, customary ruler

Name ______________________ Date ____________

Pour It On

DIRECTIONS

Collect several unmarked containers that will hold water. (Be sure to gather a variety of containers, such as milk jugs, buckets, soda bottles, milk cartons, assorted test tubes, an eyedropper, an empty prescription bottle, glasses and cups, etc.) You will also need measuring tools to measure gallons, cups, teaspoons, liters, and milliliters. Write the name of each container in the chart. Estimate how much water each container will hold, and write your estimate in the chart using the appropriate unit of measure for customary and metric measurement. Then, find the actual capacity of each container. How close were your estimates?

Measuring Capacity

Container	Customary Estimate	Metric Estimate	Customary Actual	Metric Actual

Tools: varioius containers and units of measure as suggested above; water

Name ______________________ Date ____________

Estimate Weight

DIRECTIONS

For this exercise in estimating weight, you will need a balance scale and gram weights. Gather several items from your classroom that will fit on the scale. Estimate the weight of 8 items in grams, and fill in the bar graph with your estimates in the e column using a colored pencil. Then, find the actual weight of each item, and enter that information on the graph in the a column, using a different colored pencil. How do your bars measure up?

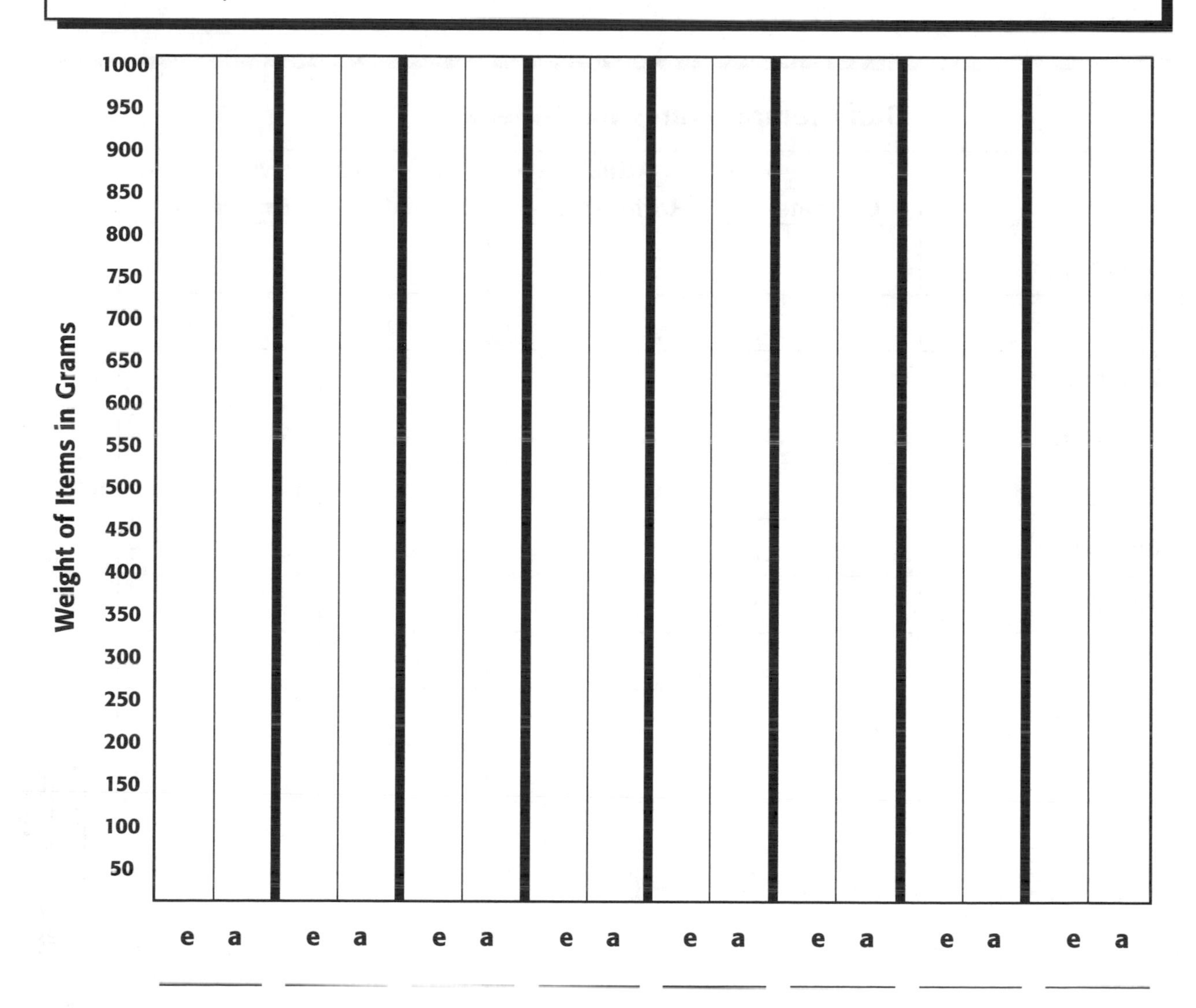

Tools: balance scale, various items as suggested above, gram weights, colored pencils

Name ______________________ Date ______________

How's the Weather?

DIRECTIONS

This exercise will cover a 2-week period. Keep a thermometer at school or at home that tells both Fahrenheit and Celsius degrees. Each day at the same time, before looking at the thermometer, estimate the temperature of the air outdoors in both Fahrenheit and Celsius degrees. Write your estimates in the chart. Then check the thermometer to find the actual temperature. Write the actual temperature in the chart. Then, calculate the difference. After 2 weeks, compare your estimates to the actual temperatures. Did your estimating skills improve?

Daily Temperatures for 2 Weeks

	°F Estimate	Actual Difference	°C Estimate	Actual Difference
Monday				
Tuesday				
Wednesday				
Thursday				
Friday				
Monday				
Tuesday				
Wednesday				
Thursday				
Friday				

Tools: thermometer that shows both Fahrenheit and Celsius degrees

Name ______________________________ Date ______________

Soup's On!

DIRECTIONS

Manuela is planning dinner. She wants to be sure that each dish will be ready in time. She decides that dinner should start with soup at 5:00 P.M. Help Manuela plan her meal. Use the information given to fill in the table. Think about whether it would be better for Manuela to overestimate or underestimate.

Dish	How Much?	Estimated Cooking Time	Starting Time	Estimated Serving Time
Soup	4 cups			
Beef	5.37 pounds			
Potatoes	4			
Beans	4 cups			
Dessert	6 baked apples			

1. The beef, potatoes, and lima beans make up the main course and should be served at the same time.
2. Manuela needs to estimate how long it will take to eat the soup so that she can figure out when to serve the main course.
3. She needs to estimate how long it will take to eat the main course so that she can figure out when to serve dessert.
4. She should allow 30–35 minutes of cooking time for each pound of beef.
5. Baking one potato takes 40 minutes. When baking more than 1 potato, allow at least 5 extra minutes for each.
6. The soup should be brought to a boil.
7. The beans are to be cooked in 2 cups of boiling water. Each cup of beans will cook for $2\frac{1}{2}$ minutes.
8. Manuela knows it takes 5 minutes for 2 cups of water to boil.
9. Baking the apples will take 40–45 minutes. They need to cool at least 15 minutes before serving.

Name ______________________ Date ____________

Curtain Call

DIRECTIONS

You are the set designer for a play. Below is a list of prices of the supplies that you need. Use this information and estimation to find the answer to each problem.

paint	$9.76 per gallon	wood	$1.68 per foot
fabric	$4.15 per yard	nails	$1.89 per box
canvas	$30.45 per roll	rope	$2.30 per yard
brushes	$5.20 each	masking tape	$0.90 per roll

1. A lumberyard has offered to supply $200.00 worth of free merchandise. Your design calls for 100 feet of wood and 12 boxes of nails. Could you get 5 more feet of wood without having to pay the lumberyard any money?

____

2. You need 76 yards of fabric and 9 rolls of canvas. The store gives a discount on any order that totals more than $600.00. How many more rolls of canvas would you have to buy to qualify for a discount?

____

3. You have brought $300.00 to the hardware store. You want to buy 21 gallons of paint, 6 brushes, and 12 rolls of masking tape. Do you have enough money to buy 30 yards of rope as well?

____

4. You wrote checks for 5 yards of fabric to Cloth Cutters, Inc., and for 10 yards of rope to Ward Hardware. You forgot to fill in the names. Which store would have received the check for the larger amount?

____

5. A friend has asked you to order some supplies for him. He wants 2 gallons of paint, one brush, and 54 feet of wood. He wants to spend about the same amount on canvas as he spends on the above items. How many rolls should you order for him?

____

6. You need 4 new curtains. Each will use 12 yards of fabric, and each will need 10 yards of rope. Your budget is $275.00. Will this be enough?

____

Name ______________________________ Date ______________

Lines, Squares, and Cubes

DIRECTIONS

Do this exercise with a partner. Fill in the Estimate Perimeter section of the table below. Then, use a customary ruler or yardstick to measure the perimeters of your desk, your teacher's desk, your classroom, and an area of your choice. Cut a square out of cardboard that measures 12 inches on a side. Use it to estimate and measure the areas of your desk, your teacher's desk, your classroom floor, and an area of your choice. Then, cut out 5 more squares, and tape them together with your first square to form a cube. Estimate and check to see how many of these cubes would fit into your classroom, your hallway, and another area of your choice. Fill in the chart.

Estimating Perimeter

	Estimate Perimeter	Estimate Area (units^2)	Estimate Volume (units^3)	Actual Perimeter	Actual Area (units^2)	Actual Volume (units^3)
Your Desk						
Teacher's Desk						
Classroom						
Hallway						
Free Choice						

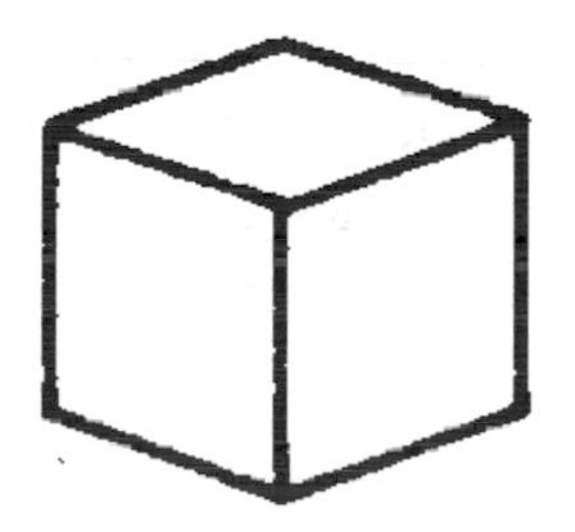

Tools: 6 12" x 12" pieces of cardboard, scissors, tape, ruler, yardstick

Name ______________________________ Date ______________

No Problem!

DIRECTIONS

Use estimation to solve each problem. Darken the circle by the correct answer.

1. If you were asked to bring 2 quarts of soda to a party, but you only had metric measurements, which measurement would be closest to 2 quarts?

Ⓐ 2 milliliters
Ⓑ 2 grams
Ⓒ 2 liters

2. The walls of a room measure 10.4 feet, 12.3 feet, 2.7 feet, 6.9 feet, 2.7 feet, 10.4 feet, 3 feet, and 3 feet. About how many feet is the perimeter of the room?

Ⓐ about 52 feet
Ⓑ about 60 feet
Ⓒ about 51 feet

3. Two friends are planning to visit Washington, D.C., for a 3-day weekend. They estimate that they will each spend about $90.00 a day. About how much money will the 2 friends need altogether for the weekend?

Ⓐ about $400
Ⓑ about $600
Ⓒ about $90

4. Leonard wants some new CDs and tapes. The tapes he wants cost $7.78 each. The CDs cost $9.98. About how much money does he need to buy 3 tapes and 2 CDs?

Ⓐ about $45.00
Ⓑ about $36.00
Ⓒ about $44.00

5. The circus has 2 elephants in a boxcar for a trip to their next stop. What is the best estimate of the weight of the elephants and the boxcar?

Ⓐ 5,000 grams
Ⓑ 5,000,000 milligrams
Ⓒ 5 metric tons

6. Josh walked along shivering and rubbing his gloved hands together. When he got to the house, he stamped his boots on the rug and closed the door quickly. Suddenly, the house felt hot and stuffy! What is the best estimate of the temperatures outside and in the house?

Ⓐ outside, 36° F; inside, 74° F
Ⓑ outside, 40° C; inside, 45° C
Ⓒ outside, 0° C; inside, 100° C

Name ______________________________ Date ______________

Unit 2 Assessment
Length

DIRECTIONS

Read each problem, and solve. Darken the circle by the correct answer.

1. Julius and his family drove to New Orleans. On the way there, they drove 298 miles. They took a shorter route back and drove 286 miles. How many miles did they drive altogether?

Ⓐ 384
Ⓑ 484
Ⓒ 584

2. Yvonne is making a new skirt to wear to the school dance. She will need $1\frac{1}{2}$ yards of fabric for the skirt and $\frac{3}{4}$ yard of ribbon for the trim. How much more fabric than ribbon trim does she need to buy?

Ⓐ $\frac{1}{6}$ yard
Ⓑ $\frac{3}{4}$ yard
Ⓒ $\frac{1}{2}$ yard

3. Joe walks a mile in 15 minutes. If Joe walks for an hour and a half, how many miles can he go?

Ⓐ 4 miles
Ⓑ 6 miles
Ⓒ 8 miles

4. Kelli wants to put fencing around her plants. She needs 11 yards of fencing. The fencing is sold in 15-foot sections. How many sections will Kelli have to buy?

Ⓐ 2 sections
Ⓑ 3 sections
Ⓒ 5 sections

5. Chuck's pencil is 5 cm long. How many times would the length of Chuck's pencil fit on a meter stick?

Ⓐ 20 times
Ⓑ 12 times
Ⓒ 10 times

6. Vinnie rides his bike 1.2 miles round trip to and from the skating rink. If he goes to the rink twice a week for 4 weeks, how many miles in all will he ride?

Ⓐ 16.8 miles
Ⓑ 10 miles
Ⓒ 9.6 miles

Go on to the next page.

Name ______________________________ Date ______________

Unit 2 Assessment

Length, p. 2

DIRECTIONS

Read each problem, and solve. Darken the circle by the correct answer.

7. How many inches are there between point B and point A?

Ⓐ $1\frac{1}{2}$ in.
Ⓑ $2\frac{1}{2}$ in.
Ⓒ $1\frac{3}{4}$ in.

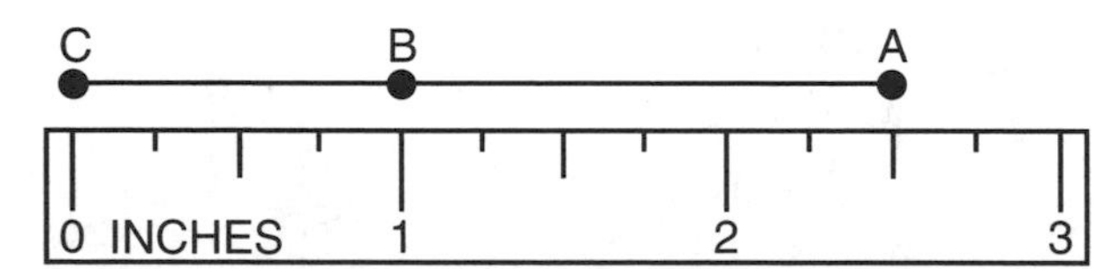

8. How many centimeters are there between point J and point L?

Ⓐ $4\frac{1}{2}$ cm
Ⓑ 6 cm
Ⓒ 5 cm

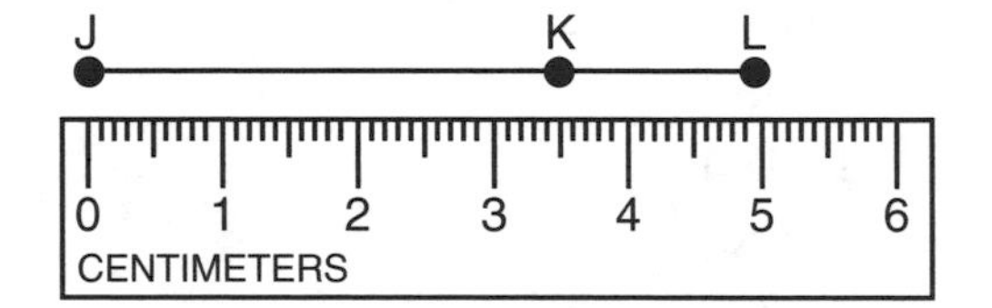

9. Cam's index finger is about 8 cm long. If Cam is 2 meters and 4 cm tall, how many fingers tall would he be?

Ⓐ $12\frac{1}{2}$ fingers
Ⓑ $25\frac{1}{2}$ fingers
Ⓒ $50\frac{1}{2}$ fingers

10. Dharma's favorite race is the 500-yard dash. She holds the record for her school. How many feet does she run?

Ⓐ 1,500 feet
Ⓑ 150 feet
Ⓒ 5,000 feet

11. Tara's hair grows about 1 inch every month. If she has 3 inches cut off every other month, what will be the difference in the length of her hair at the end of 1 year?

Ⓐ 3 inches shorter
Ⓑ 6 inches shorter
Ⓒ 6 inches longer

12. Kelsey is running in a 10-kilometer race. She has already run 7 kilometers. How many more meters will she have to run before she can finish the race?

Ⓐ 3 meters
Ⓑ 3,000 meters
Ⓒ 300 meters

Name ______________________ Date ______________

This Tool Rules

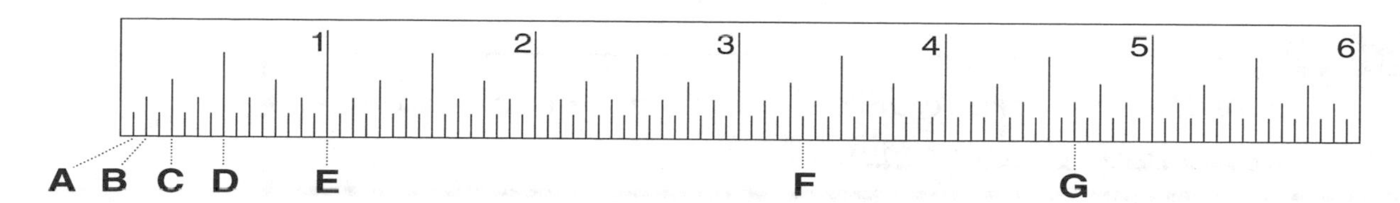

This is a section of a customary ruler. It measures length. The markings on the ruler divide it into inches. Each inch is divided into halves, quarters, eighths, and sixteenths.

- The **A** above shows $\frac{1}{16}$ of 1 inch.
- The **B** above shows $\frac{1}{8}$ of 1 inch.
- The **C** above shows $\frac{1}{4}$ of one inch.
- The **D** above shows $\frac{1}{2}$ of one inch.
- The **E** above shows 1 inch exactly.
- What does the **F** show? How many inches does it show? How many parts of an inch? If you say $3\frac{5}{16}$ inches, you are right.
- What does the **G** show? ______________

DIRECTIONS

Look at the ruler below. For each letter, write the measurement that is shown.

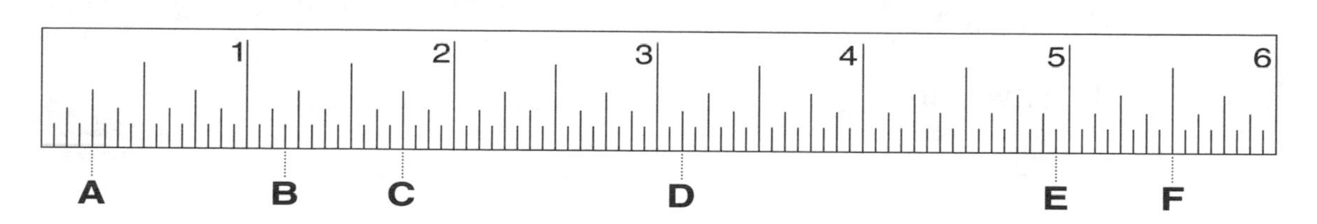

A. ______ **B.** ______ **C.** ______ **D.** ______ **E.** ______ **F.** ______

DIRECTIONS

Use a customary ruler to find the length of each item to the nearest $\frac{1}{16}$ of an inch.

1. ______________

2. ______________

3. ______________

Tool: customary ruler

Name ______________________________ Date ______________

Use Your Head!

DIRECTIONS

Choose the appropriate unit of measure for each example. Write inches, feet, yards, or miles.

1. the distance an airplane travels ______________________

2. the length of a chalkboard ______________________

3. the length of a book ______________________

4. the height of a child ______________________

5. the distance from one town to another ______________________

6. the height of a cat ______________________

7. the height of a tree ______________________

8. the length of a finger ______________________

9. the width of a room ______________________

10. the height of a mountain ______________________

11. the length of a sports field ______________________

12. the length of a fence ______________________

13. the height of a skyscraper ______________________

14. the depth of a well ______________________

15. the depth of the ocean ______________________

16. the length of a person's hair ______________________

17. the length of a bicycle race ______________________

18. the distance a pitcher throws a baseball ______________________

19. the width of a smile ______________________

20. the width of a car ______________________

Go on to the next page.

Name ______________________ Date ______________

Use Your Head!, p. 2

DIRECTIONS

Choose the appropriate unit of measure for each example.
Write millimeters, centimeters, decimeters, meters, or kilometers.

21. the length of a cross-country drive ______________

22. the length of an ant ______________

23. the height of an adult ______________

24. the depth of a canyon ______________

25. the distance a person can kick a soccer ball ______________

26. the length of a ball court ______________

27. the width of a pencil ______________

28. the length of a picture frame ______________

29. the length of an envelope ______________

30. the depth of a bathtub ______________

31. the length of a classroom ______________

32. the height of a mountain ______________

33. the distance traveled by a train ______________

34. the length of a hose ______________

35. the diameter of a drop of water ______________

36. the diameter of a CD ______________

37. the distance from one classroom to another ______________

38. the length of a postal worker's route ______________

39. the length of a book ______________

40. the length of a straw ______________

Name ______________________ Date ______________

The Long and Short of It

DIRECTIONS

Measure each line segment to the part of the inch that gives the most precise measurement.

1. __________
2. __________
3. __________
4. __________

DIRECTIONS

Draw a line to the given length.

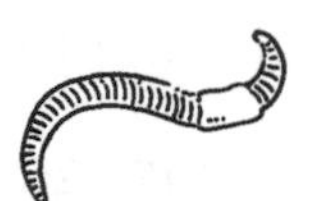

5. $1\frac{1}{2}$ in. •
6. $2\frac{1}{8}$ in. •
7. $3\frac{1}{4}$ in. •
8. $\frac{9}{16}$ in. •

DIRECTIONS

Complete each sentence.

9. 2 ft = _______ in.
10. 1.5 mi = _______ yd
11. 50 yd = _______ ft
12. 24 in. = _______ ft
13. 2,640 ft = _______ yd
14. 12 ft = _______ yd
15. 5,280 yd = _______ mi
16. 108 in. = _______ yd
17. 15,840 ft = _______ mi

DIRECTIONS

Write the number sentence, and solve this problem.

18. Bayard is 5 ft $5\frac{3}{4}$ in. tall. Jose is 5 ft $5\frac{9}{16}$ in. tall. Who is taller? How much taller is he?

____

Go on to the next page.

Tools: customary ruler

Name ______________________________ Date ______________

The Long and Short of It, p. 2

DIRECTIONS

Measure each line segment to the most precise metric measurement.

19. __________

20. __________

21. __________

22. __________

DIRECTIONS

Draw a line to the given length.

23. $5\frac{1}{2}$ cm •

24. 37 mm •

25. 1 dm •

26. 3 cm •

DIRECTIONS

Complete each sentence.

27. 10 mm = ______ cm

28. 100 cm = ______ dm

29. 1,000 dm = ______ m

30. 20 dm = ______ m

31. 1,000 mm = ______ cm

32. 5 dm = ______ m

33. 1 km = ______ m

34. 1 cm – ______ m

35. 1,000 mm = ______ m

DIRECTIONS

Write the number sentence, and solve this problem.

36. A vine grew 6 cm the first week, 4.3 cm the second week, 5.1 cm the third week, and 7.8 cm the fourth week. How many cm did it grow altogether?

____

Tools: metric ruler

Name ______________________________ Date ______________

Measure the Miles

DIRECTIONS

The scale on a map is the relationship between distance on a map and actual distance. For example, a scale of 1 inch to 3 miles means that 1 inch on the map is equal to 3 miles of actual distance. On this map, the scale is written in the lower right corner. Use the map to answer the questions.

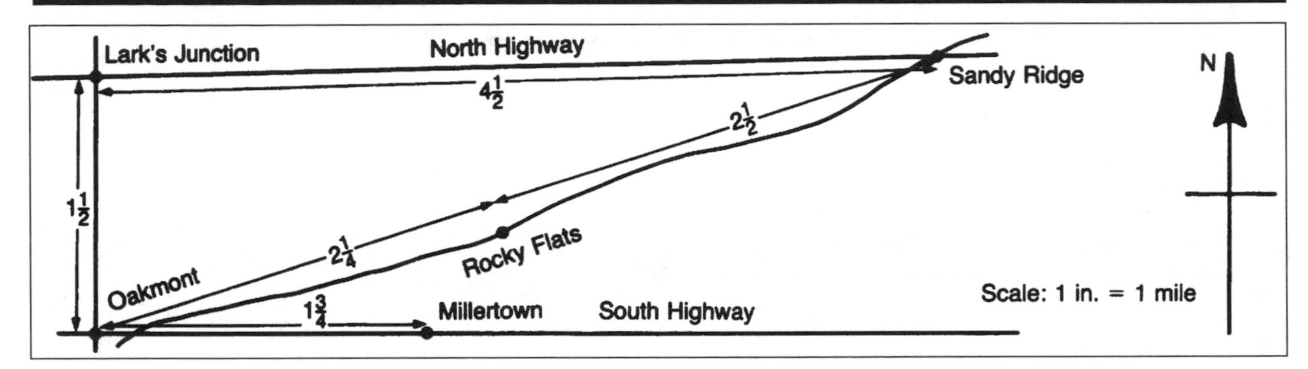

1. At Oakmont, North Highway and South Highway are $1\frac{1}{2}$ inches apart. How far apart are they actually?

____

2. Lark's Junction and Sandy Ridge are $4\frac{1}{2}$ inches apart. How far apart are they actually?

____

3. If you traveled from Lark's Junction to Oakmont, then from Oakmont to Sandy Ridge, how far would you go actually?

____

4. Which towns would you pass through if you took the shortest route from Sandy Ridge to Millertown? How far would you go?

____

Maps have many different scales. One inch on the map might equal several miles of actual distance. Suppose that the map above had a scale of 1 inch = 50 miles.

5. How far apart would North Highway and South Highway actually be?

____

6. How far apart would Sandy Ridge and Oakmont actually be?

____

7. How far apart would Oakmont and Millertown actually be?

____

8. What would be the actual distance from Lark's Junction to Sandy Ridge?

____

Name ______________________ Date ______________

Work It Out

DIRECTIONS

Read each problem, and solve.

1. During his vacation, Mr. Weiss will hike 152 miles along the Appalachian Trail. He plans to walk the same distance each day. How far must Mr. Weiss hike daily to complete the hike in 8 days?

____

2. John buys rope that is 36 feet long. He cuts it into 12 equal pieces so his scout troop can practice tying different kinds of knots. How long is each piece of rope?

____

3. Ms. Ramirez buys new tires. The tires are under warranty for 35,000 miles. She has already driven 27,248 miles. How many warranty miles does she have left on these tires?

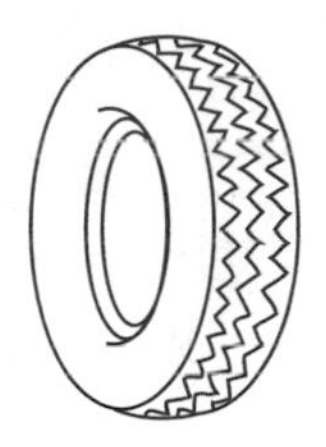

____

4. Carl drives 36.7 kilometers to work. How many kilometers does he drive round-trip?

____

5. Roger is a traveling salesman. One year, he drives 107,345 miles. The next year, he drives 98,416 miles. The third year, he drives 123,450 miles. What is the average number of miles Roger drives per year?

____

6. For a costume party, Maria decides to dress up as a potted fern. She buys a roll of foam rubber 12 meters long and 1 meter wide. It takes 2 meters of foam rubber to make 1 leaf. How many leaves can she make and still have 2 meters left for the base of her costume?

____

7. Mark decides to dress as his favorite food. He makes meatballs out of papier mâché and noodles out of ribbon. The ribbon comes in spools 8 yards long. If Mark makes each noodle 6 feet long, how many spools of ribbon will he need to make 45 noodles?

____

Name ______________________ Date ______________

See the Sights

DIRECTIONS

Look at a map of the Unites States. Find a place you would like to visit. Estimate that you can drive an average of 55 miles per hour, and you can get 28 miles per gallon of gas. How long will it actually take to travel to this place? How many gallons of gas will you use to get there? Figure out where you will need to stop for gas. List the states and large cities you will pass through, where you will need to stop for gas, and where you will stop to spend the night, if necessary.

Tools: U.S. road map, calculator

Name ______________________ Date ______________

Unit 3 Assessment
Capacity

DIRECTIONS

Read each problem, and solve. Darken the circle by the correct answer.

1. What would be the best unit to use to measure the amount of cider in a drinking glass?

Ⓐ teaspoon
Ⓑ cup
Ⓒ quart

2. Which measurement would describe the amount of medicine in a dropper?

Ⓐ 6 liters
Ⓑ 6 milliliters
Ⓒ 6 kiloliters

3. Jerry needs 5 quarts of paint to cover the walls of his kitchen. The color he likes is only available in gallon cans. How many cans will Jerry need to buy?

Ⓐ 4 cans
Ⓑ 16 cans
Ⓒ 2 cans

4. How many milliliters are there in a 2-liter bottle of soda?

Ⓐ 2,000 mL
Ⓑ 200 mL
Ⓒ 20,000 mL

5. Mrs. Kahn adds 2 cups of water to each container of dry paint for art class. If she has 12 different colors of paint, how many pints of water will she need to get all of the paint ready?

Ⓐ 4 pints
Ⓑ 8 pints
Ⓒ 12 pints

6. The Howe family drinks 2 quarts of orange juice every week. How many gallons of juice do the Howes drink in a 4-week month?

Ⓐ 4 gallons
Ⓑ 2 gallons
Ⓒ 10 gallons

Go on to the next page.

Name ______________________________ Date ______________

Unit 3 Assessment

Capacity, p. 2

DIRECTIONS

Read each problem, and solve. Darken the circle by the correct answer.

7. Debra bought strawberries for a fruit salad. What amount did she probably buy?

Ⓐ 1 tablespoon
Ⓑ 1 quart
Ⓒ 1 gallon

8. Paula is making 5 blueberry pies for a bake sale. She needs 4 cups of blueberries for each pie. She has picked 4 quarts of blueberries. How many more quarts does she need to make all 5 pies?

Ⓐ 1 more quart
Ⓑ 4 more quarts
Ⓒ no more quarts

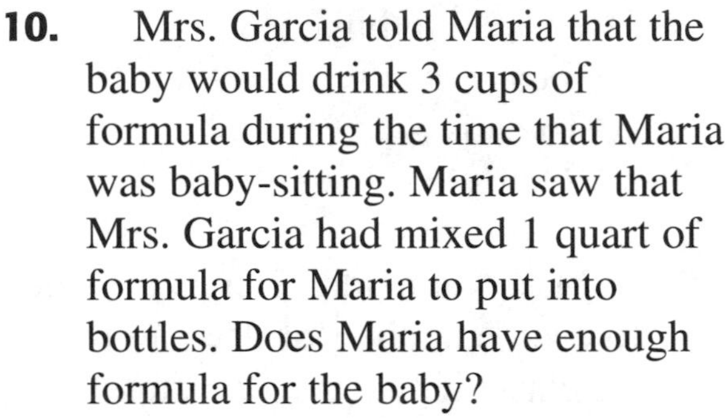

9. Martin's Grocery is selling orange juice for $3.95 a gallon. DeWitt's is selling orange juice for $1.00 a quart. Which store has the better price on orange juice?

Ⓐ They are both the same.
Ⓑ Martin's Grocery
Ⓒ DeWitt's

10. Mrs. Garcia told Maria that the baby would drink 3 cups of formula during the time that Maria was baby-sitting. Maria saw that Mrs. Garcia had mixed 1 quart of formula for Maria to put into bottles. Does Maria have enough formula for the baby?

Ⓐ No, she needs 1 more cup.
Ⓑ Yes, she has an extra cup.
Ⓒ Yes, she has the exact amount she needs.

11. Dana drinks 800 mL of water every day. How much water does he drink in 5 days?

Ⓐ 8 L
Ⓑ 2 L
Ⓒ 4 L

12. Jailea uses 2 tablespoons of cocoa powder for each 2-cup mug of hot chocolate she makes. How many tablespoons will she need to make hot chocolate for a group of 12 people?

Ⓐ 24 tbsp
Ⓑ 12 tbsp
Ⓒ 6 tbsp

Name ______________________________ Date ________________

Choose Your Measure

DIRECTIONS

Choose the more reasonable estimate of capacity. Circle a or b.

1. glass of water

a. 2 cups
b. 2 pints

2. watering can

a. 2 quarts
b. 2 tablespoons

3. medicine dropper

a. $\frac{1}{4}$ teaspoon
b. $\frac{1}{4}$ cup

4. aquarium

a. 10 cups
b. 10 gallons

DIRECTIONS

Choose the more reasonable unit of measure. Write tsp, c, qt, or gal.

5. swimming pool

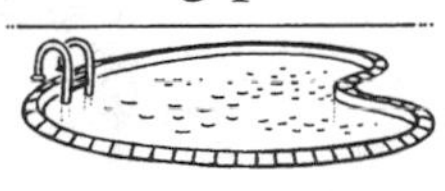

____

6. milk carton

____

7. thimble

____

8. cooler

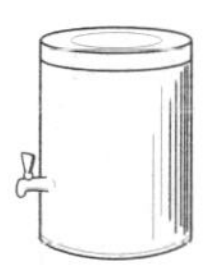

____

9. juice box

____

10. paint tube

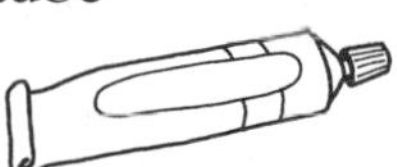

____

DIRECTIONS

Complete each sentence.

11. 8 pints = __________ quarts

12. 1 gallon = __________ cups

13. 6 cups = __________ pints

14. 16 quarts = __________ gallons

DIRECTIONS

Solve this problem.

15. A pizza shop sells 1 gallon of lemonade for \$2.09, a quart of lemonade for \$0.79, and 1 pint of lemonade for \$0.25. Which is the best way to buy 1 gallon of lemonade?

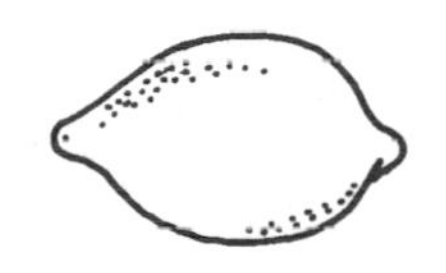

____

Go on to the next page.

Name ______________________________ Date ______________

Choose Your Measure, p.2

DIRECTIONS

Choose the more reasonable estimate of capacity. Circle a or b.

16. cup of tea — **a.** 250 mL **b.** 250 L

17. paint bucket — **a.** 2 mL **b.** 2 L

18. contact lens case — **a.** 40 mL **b.** 40 L

19. bathtub — **a.** 200 mL **b.** 200 L

DIRECTIONS

Choose the more reasonable unit of measure. Write mL or L.

20. fish tank

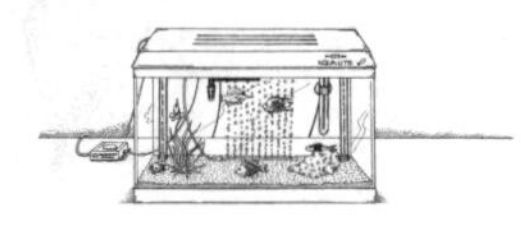

____

21. glass

____

22. large pot

____

23. trash barrel

____

24. thimble

____

25. swimming pool

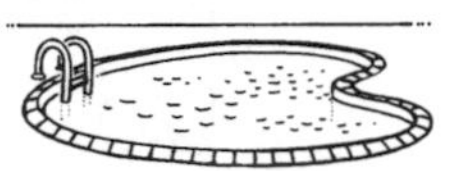

____

DIRECTIONS

Complete each sentence.

26. 2.091 L = 2,091 __________

27. 16,000 mL = 16 __________

28. 50.5 mL = __________ L

29. 406.2 L = __________ mL

DIRECTIONS

Solve this problem.

30. Kyle is making lemonade from a powdered mix. The container says one scoop of powder will make 0.75 L. How many scoops are needed to make 3 L?

____

Name ______________________________ Date ______________

Another Way to Say It

DIRECTIONS

Write multiply or divide.

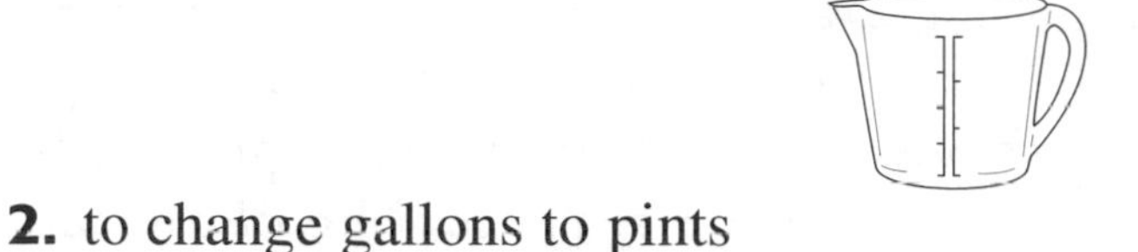

1. to change cups to gallons

____

2. to change gallons to pints

____

3. to change pints to cups

____

4. to change quarts to gallons

____

5. to change tablespoons to cups

____

6. to change quarts to pints

____

DIRECTIONS

Complete each sentence.

7. 24 qt = ______ gal

8. 12 qt = ______ c

9. 7 pt = ______ c

10. 4 c = ______ fl oz

11. 24 pt = ______ qt

12. $2\frac{3}{4}$ gal = ______ qt

13. 4 gal = ______ qt

14. 3 gal = ______ pt

15. 8 qt = ______ pt

16. $2\frac{1}{2}$ pt = ______ c

17. $4\frac{1}{2}$ pt = ______ qt

18. 5 gal = ______ pt

19. $\frac{3}{4}$ gal = ______ c

20. 16 fl oz = ______ c

21. 3 tbsp = ______ tsp

DIRECTIONS

Write the number sentence, and solve this problem.

22. Ella's doctor told her she should drink 2.5 gal of water every week during the summer. How many 8-oz glasses of water should she drink in a week?

____

Name ______________________ Date ______________

Cooking for a Crowd

DIRECTIONS

A recipe shows how many people it is meant to serve. When it serves more people, then the amount of the ingredients must be changed in proportion to the number of people it will serve. Change the amounts of the ingredients of each recipe. Write fractions in their simplest form.

Cheese Bake
(Serves 3)
1 c flour
$1\frac{1}{2}$ tsp baking powder
$\frac{1}{2}$ tsp salt
2 tsp butter
$\frac{1}{2}$ c grated cheddar cheese
$\frac{1}{3}$ c cold water

Cheese Bake
(Serves 8)
______ c flour
______ tsp baking powder
______ tsp salt
______ tsp butter
______ c grated cheddar cheese
______ c cold water

Potato Delight
(Serves 4)
2 c bread crumbs
4 eggs
14 oz evaporated milk
1 tsp onion powder
3 tsp salt
$1\frac{1}{2}$ tbsp Worcestershire sauce
4 potatoes
8 oz frozen vegetables
5 raw carrots
7 oz gravy

Potato Delight
(Serves 14)
______ c bread crumbs
______ eggs
______ oz evaporated milk
______ tsp onion powder
______ tsp salt
______ tbsp Worcestershire sauce
______ potatoes
______ oz frozen vegetables
______ raw carrots
______ oz gravy

Name ______________________ Date ______________

A Way with Words

DIRECTIONS Read each problem, and solve.

1. A recipe calls for $2\frac{1}{4}$ cups of flour. The recipe makes 8 servings. How many cups of flour will be needed to make 24 servings?

____

2. John's mother bought a 2-liter bottle of apple juice. John and his brothers drank 0.75 liter of juice. How much was left in the jar?

____

3. Henry is in charge of serving punch at the school picnic. Each punch cup holds 245 milliliters. He needs to fill 14 punch cups. How much punch will he need?

____

4. Laura used $\frac{3}{4}$ cup of milk for a pudding recipe, $\frac{1}{2}$ cup of milk for a cake recipe, and $\frac{1}{4}$ cup of milk for whipped potatoes. How many cups of milk did she use altogether?

____

5. Sophie needs 12 ounces of molasses for a recipe. What fractional part of a pint does she need?

____

6. A normal heart can pump 23.5 liters of blood through the body every 5 minutes. How many liters of blood can the heart pump in 1 minute?

____

7. A recipe for cookies calls for 1 teaspoon of vanilla to make 5 dozen cookies. How many cookies could you make if you increased the recipe to use 1 tablespoon of vanilla?

____

8. Sam gives each of the 12 plants in his windows 1 cup of water every 6 days. How many days would it take Sam to use exactly 6 gallons of water on his plants?

____

Go on to the next page.

Name ______________________ Date ______________

A Way with Words, p. 2

DIRECTIONS

Read each problem, and solve.

9. Jason uses $\frac{1}{2}$ cup of detergent to do each load of laundry. If he buys a bottle of detergent that holds 2.8 gallons, how many loads of laundry can he do?

____

10. Lara used about 2 ounces of water for each clay pot she made in art class. If Lara made 5 pots, did she use more or less than a cup of water?

____

11. Dana collects 2 vials of water from the lake near her home each day for testing. Each vial holds 35 mL. How many L of water will Dana have collected after 30 days?

____

12. A maple tree is dripping sap into a bucket at the rate of about 2 tsp per minute. How long will it take the tree to fill the bucket with 22 tbsp of sap?

____

13. A rain barrel collected 3.6 L of water in 1 month. If the month had 30 days, what was the average amount of rainwater in mL collected each day?

____

14. A pool holds 15,000 gallons of water. A pool service has drained 12,468 gallons of water from the pool in order to repair the lining. How many gallons of water are left in the pool?

____

15. Each of the 4 walls of Kareem's room is the same size. He uses $1\frac{1}{2}$ quarts of paint to cover 1 wall. How much paint will he need to do the whole room?

____

16. If the paint that Kareem used came only in gallons, how many would he have to buy?

____

Name ______________________________ Date ______________

Mix and Measure

DIRECTIONS

Find a recipe for a fruit drink or punch in a cookbook or on the Internet. Write the recipe below, and then write the list of ingredients for 5 times the amount of the drink.

To make the drink for your family, would you need to use the recipe as it is, or would you want to use smaller amounts? Make the drink for your family using either the original recipe amounts or a fraction of the original amounts, depending on the size of your family.

Original Recipe	**Recipe × 5**	**Recipe for Your Family**

Tools: cookbook or Internet, pitcher, units of measure as directed in recipe, recipe ingredients

Name ______________________ Date ____________

Wet Your Whistle

DIRECTIONS

Doctors recommend that people drink at least 8 8-ounce glasses of water each day. Do you drink enough water?

Find a water bottle or a covered drinking container that you can carry with you throughout the day. (A canning jar or a glass will work, but plastic is safer.) Measure the amount of water that it will hold. Keep track of how many times you fill the glass or bottle during the day. Make sure that you know how much water you are putting in the bottle. At the end of the day, add the number of bottles that you drank for your total. If there is water left in your bottle, measure it, and subtract that amount from your total.

How did you measure up? Try it again for a second day, and see if you can improve your water-drinking habits.

Day 1 **Day 2**

Tools: water bottle, measuring cup, water

Name ______________________________ Date ______________

Unit 4 Assessment

Temperature

DIRECTIONS

Read each problem, and solve. Darken the circle by the correct answer.

1. Which temperature does the thermometer show?

Ⓐ 45° F
Ⓑ 50° F
Ⓒ 47° F

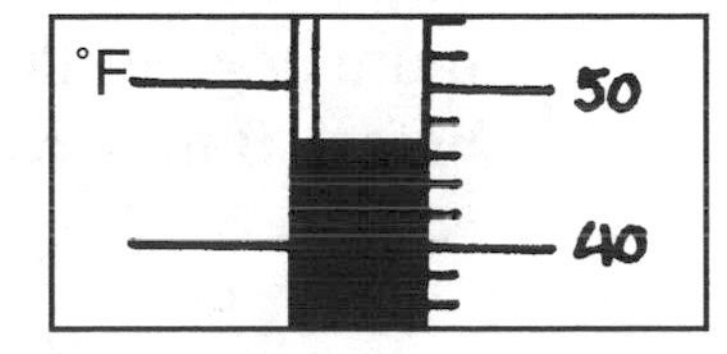

2. Which temperature does the thermometer show?

Ⓐ 12° F
Ⓑ 10° F
Ⓒ 15° F

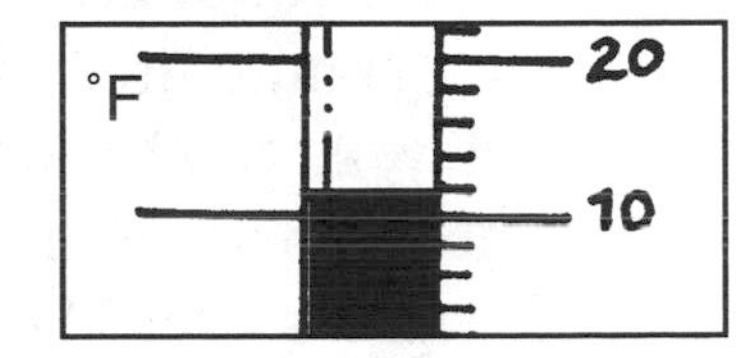

3. Which temperature does the thermometer show?

Ⓐ 90° F
Ⓑ 93° F
Ⓒ 92° F

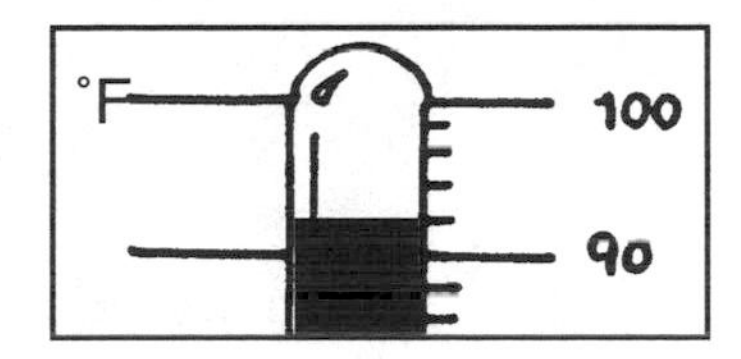

4. Which temperature does the thermometer show?

Ⓐ 30° C
Ⓑ 3° C
Ⓒ 5° C

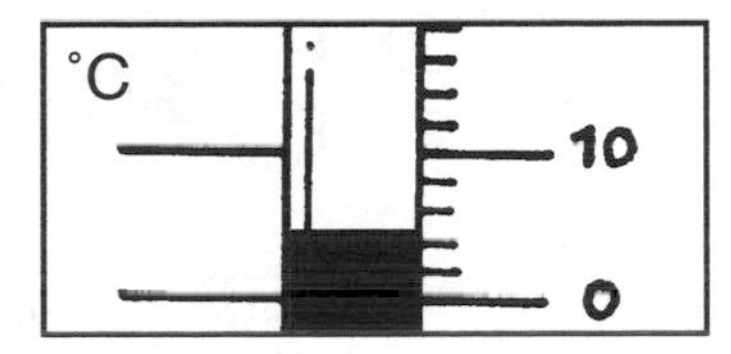

5. Which temperature does the thermometer show?

Ⓐ 15° C
Ⓑ 20° C
Ⓒ 5° C

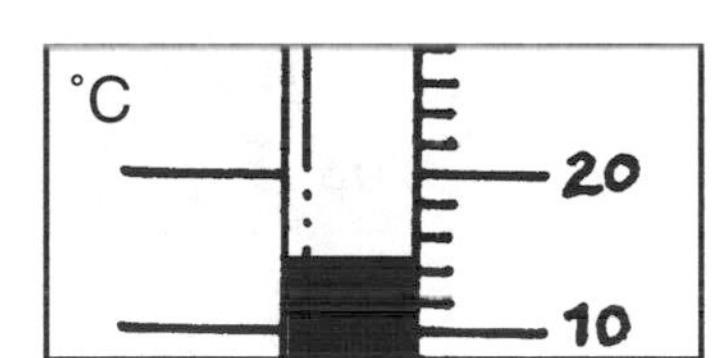

6. Which temperature does the thermometer show?

Ⓐ 30° C
Ⓑ 45° C
Ⓒ 35° C

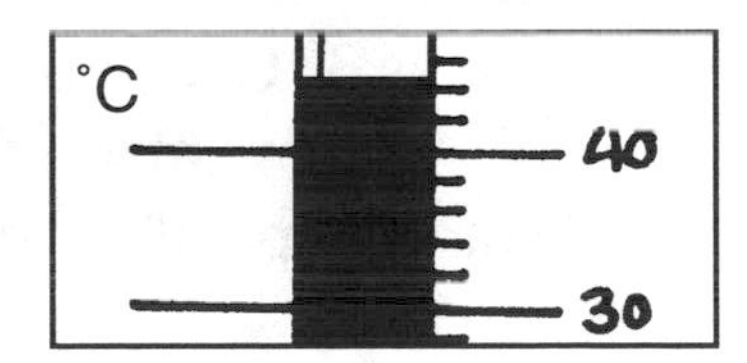

Go on to the next page.

Name ______________________________ Date ______________

Unit 4 Assessment

Temperature, p. 2

DIRECTIONS

Read each problem, and solve. Darken the circle by the correct answer.

7. The students at Carver Elementary School will not go outside for afternoon recess if the temperature drops below 25° F today. At 8:00 A.M., it was 32° F. The temperature has been dropping 2 degrees every hour. If it continues to drop at this rate, what will the temperature be at 1:00 P.M. when it is time for afternoon recess?

Ⓐ 42° F
Ⓑ 22° F
Ⓒ 24° F

8. Bailey is making cookies that should bake at 375° F. His oven has heated to 220° F. How many more degrees does it need to heat before Bailey can put in a tray of cookies?

Ⓐ 145° F
Ⓑ 255° F
Ⓒ 155° F

9. Mr. Garfield can only paint outside if it is above freezing. On Monday, the temperature was -5° C, on Tuesday, it was 0° C, on Wednesday it was 5° C, on Thursday it was 3° C, and on Friday it was -2° C. How many days could Mr. Garfield paint outside this week?

Ⓐ 1 day
Ⓑ 2 days
Ⓒ 3 days

10. What would be the best estimate of the temperature of a cup of hot tea?

Ⓐ 150° F
Ⓑ 212° F
Ⓒ 68° F

11. Bart says that his thermometer reaches the boiling point at 212° F. Howie says that his thermometer reaches the boiling point at 100° C. Which boy is correct?

Ⓐ Bart
Ⓑ Rick
Ⓒ Both of them

12. The temperature outside is 58° F. What type of activity should Cheryl plan with her friends?

Ⓐ volleyball on the beach
Ⓑ hiking up a mountain
Ⓒ ice-skating on the town pond

Name ______________________ Date ______________

Hot and Cold

DIRECTIONS Read each thermometer, and write the temperature shown in Fahrenheit degrees.

1. 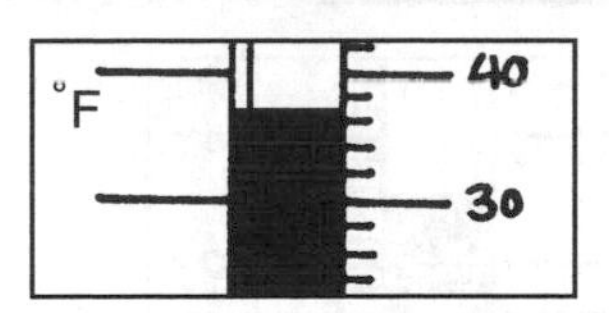

____

2. 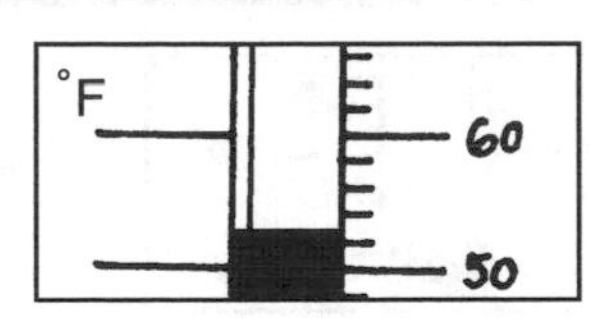

____

3. 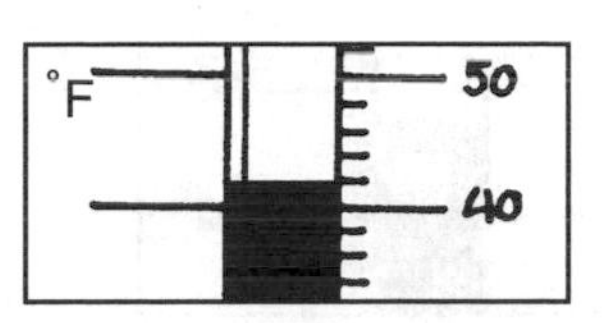

____

4. 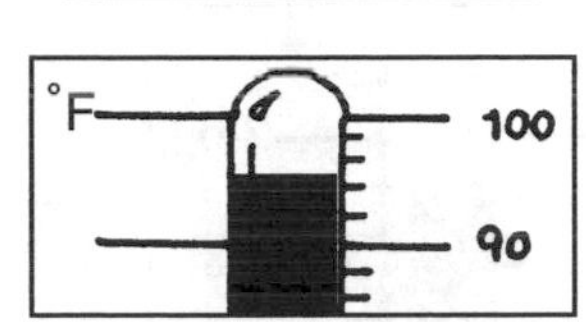

____

5. 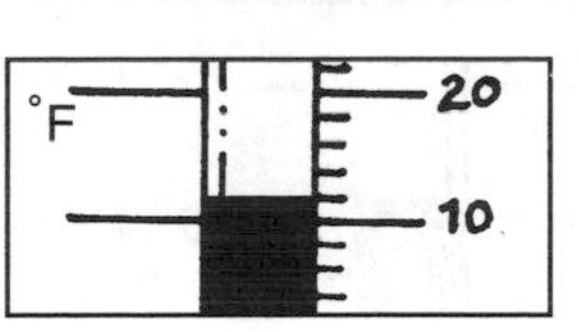

____

6. 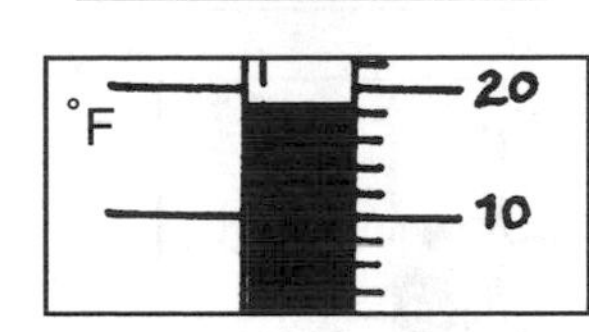

____

DIRECTIONS Fill in each thermometer to show the temperature written.

7. 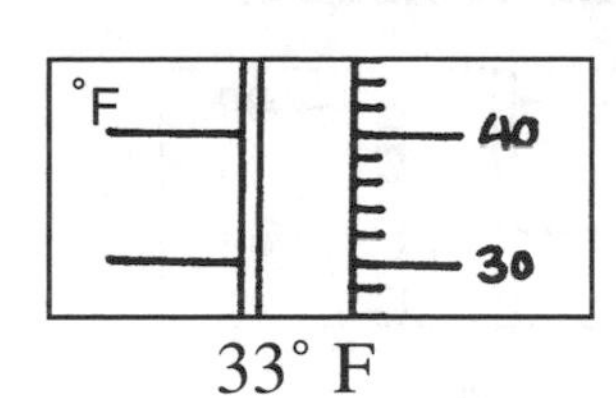

33° F

8. 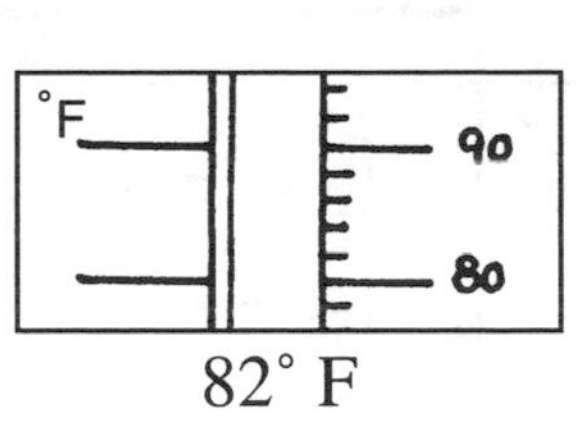

82° F

9. 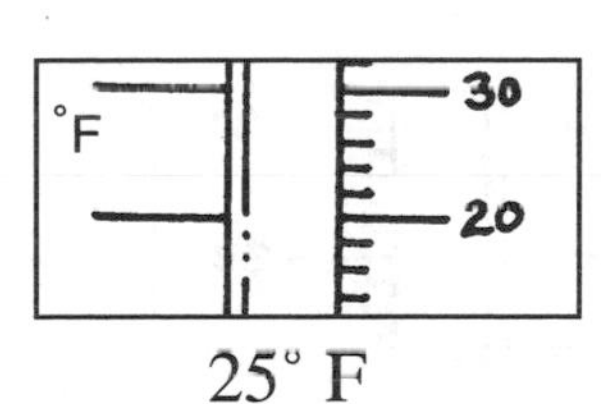

25° F

10. 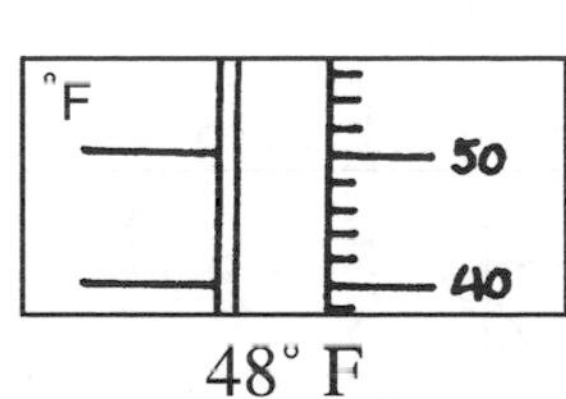

48° F

11. 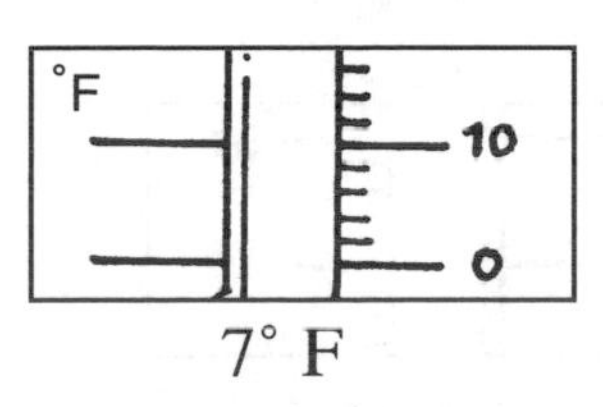

7° F

12. 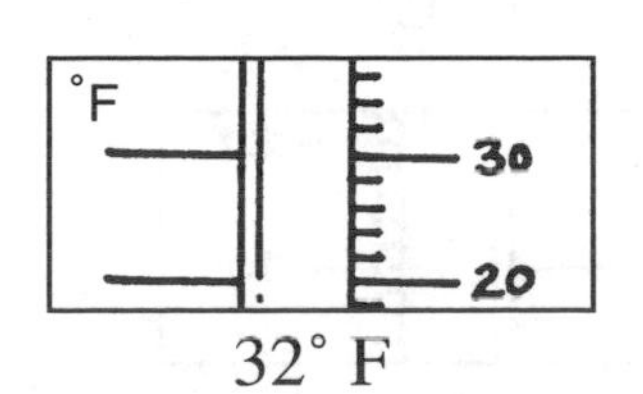

32° F

Go on to the next page.

Name ______________________ Date ______________

Hot and Cold, p. 2

DIRECTIONS

Read each thermometer, and write the temperature shown in Celsius degrees.

13. 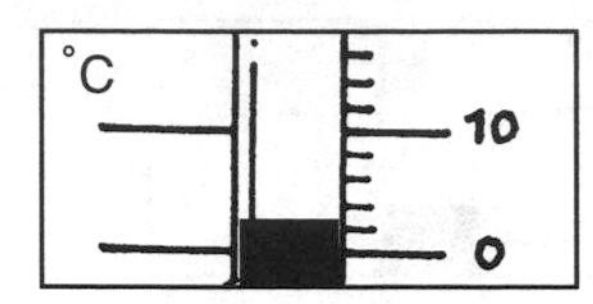

____

14. 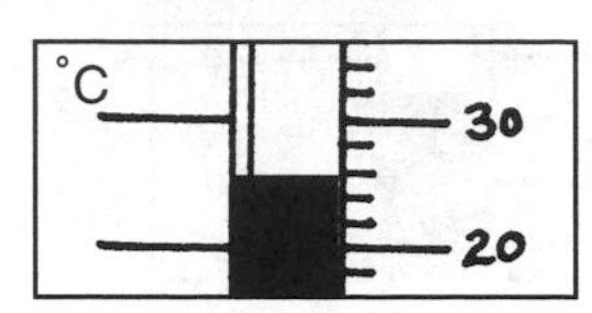

____

15. 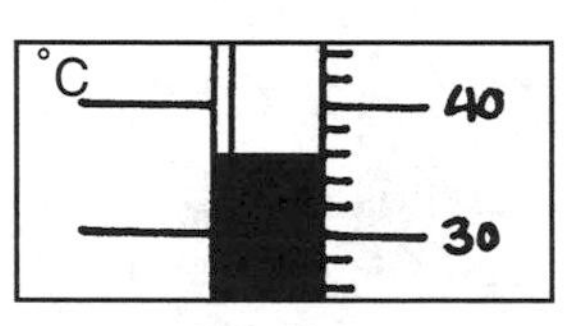

____

16. 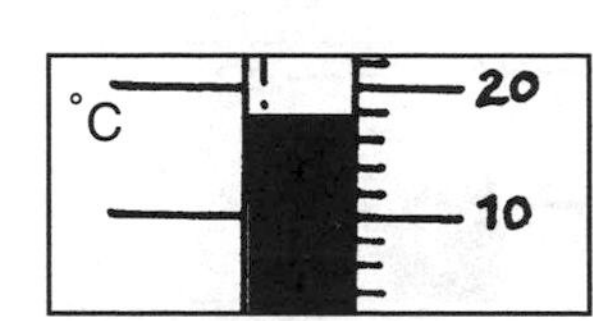

____

17. 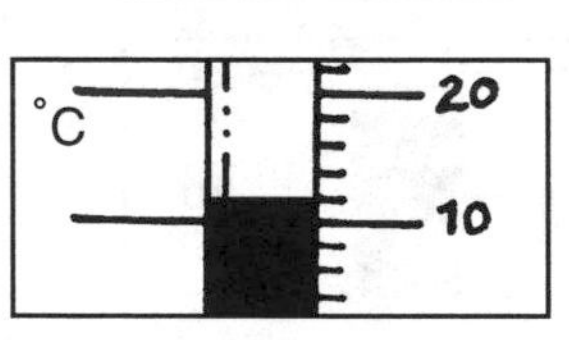

____

18. 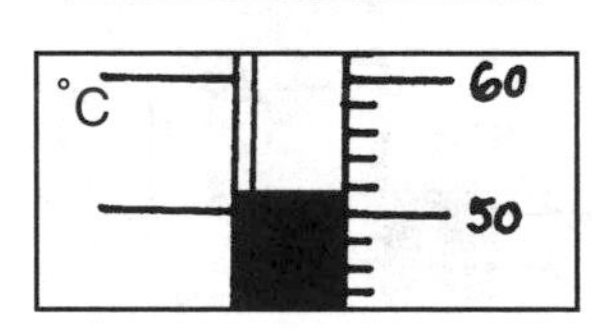

____

DIRECTIONS

Fill in each thermometer to show the temperature written.

19. 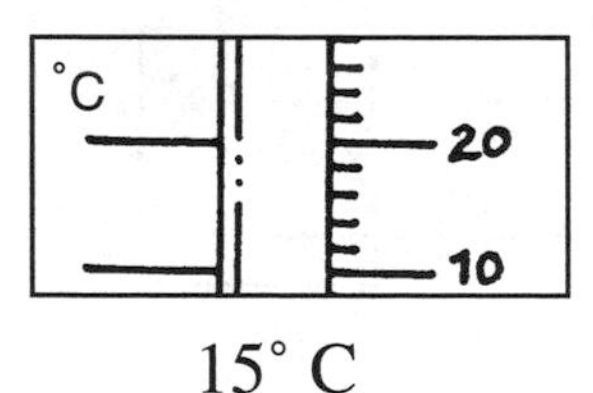

15° C

20. 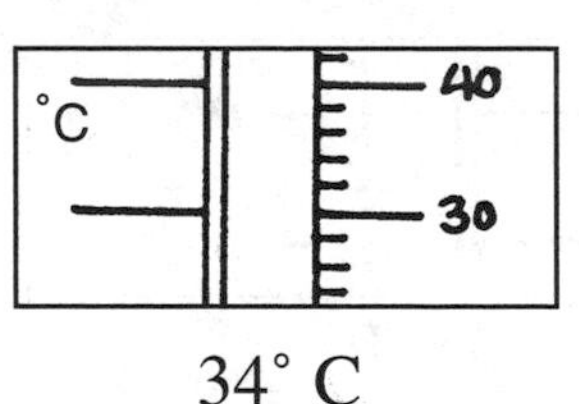

34° C

21. 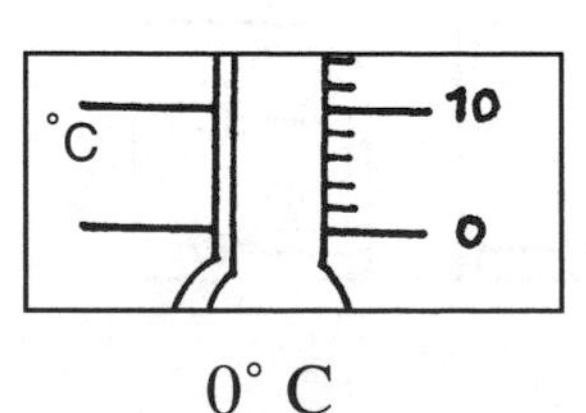

0° C

22. 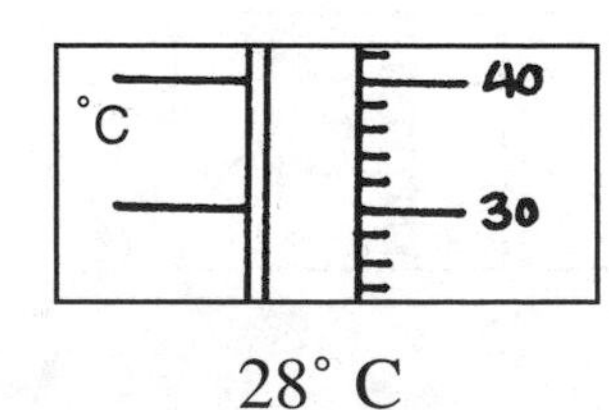

28° C

23. 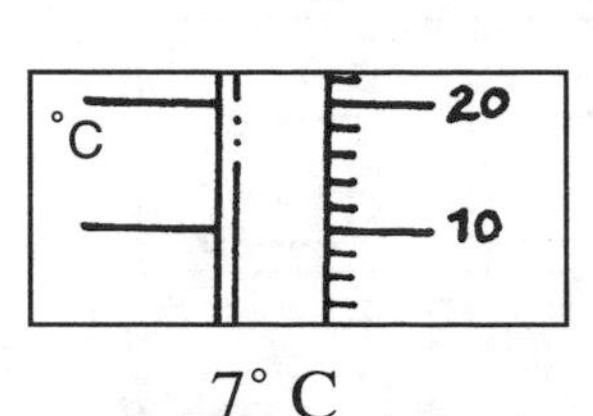

7° C

24. 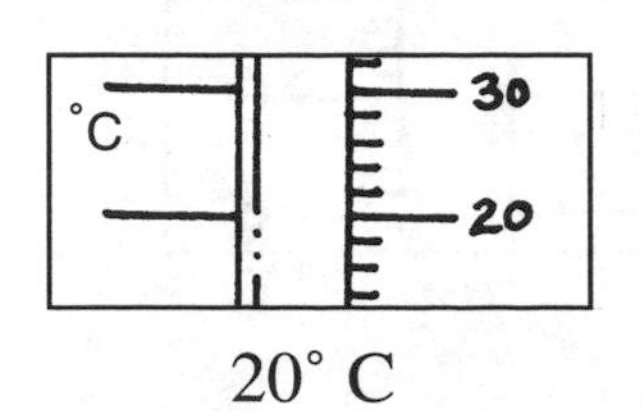

20° C

Name ______________________ Date ____________

Cold Snap

DIRECTIONS

Use the line graph for Exercises 1–4.

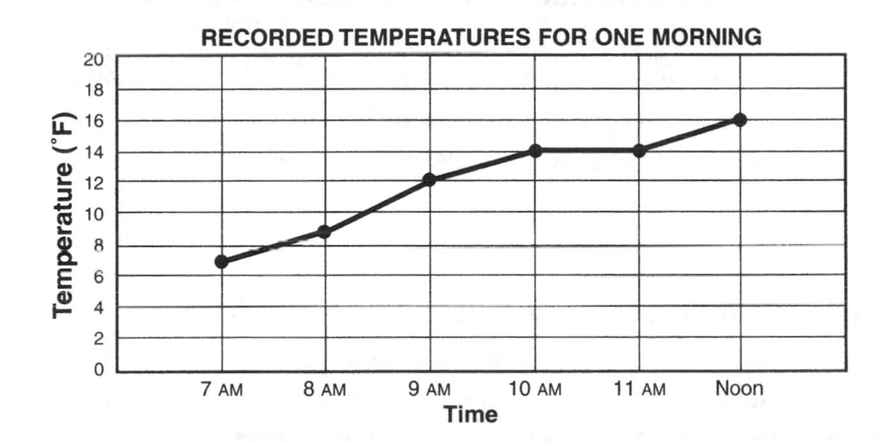

1. At what time was the highest temperature recorded?

   ____

2. At which 2 times was the same temperature recorded?

   ____

3. About what temperature was it at 8 A.M.?

   ____

4. Between which 2 hours was the greatest increase in temperature recorded?

   ____

DIRECTIONS

Make a line graph to show the data on the table. Choose a scale, title, and label for your graph.

Average Temperature	
Month	**Temperature**
July	78° F
August	84° F
September	72° F
October	65° F
November	42° F

Name ______________________________ Date ______________

Ski Weeks

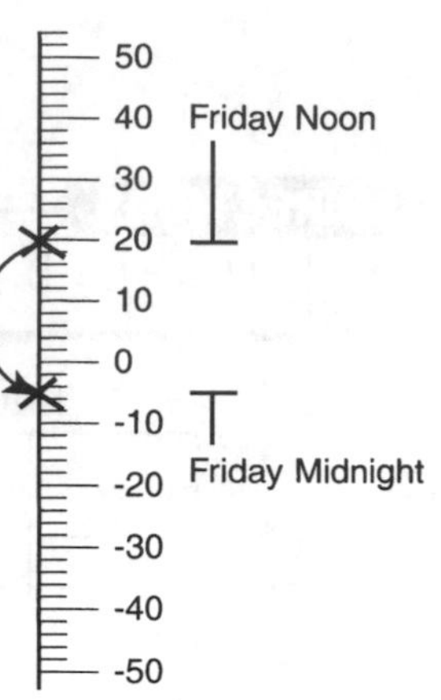

At 0 degrees on the Celsius scale, water turns into ice. Any temperature warmer than 0° is shown by numbers like 5° or 20°. Any temperature colder than 0° is shown by numbers like -5° or -20°. Zero separates numbers like 1, 2, 3, 4 from numbers like -1, -2, -3, -4.

Last winter the Carters rented a ski cabin in the mountains. The thermometer showed 20° when the Carters arrived on Friday at noon. By midnight, the thermometer showed -5°. The temperature had fallen by 25°.

DIRECTIONS

Show how the temperature changed on each of the next 4 days. Mark an X by both temperatures on the thermometer. Then, write how many degrees the temperature changed from noon to midnight.

1. Saturday
Noon: -5°

Saturday
Midnight: -20°

Change: ______

°C 30 20 10 0 -10 -20 -30

2. Sunday
Noon: 10°

Sunday
Midnight: -20°

Change: ______

°C 30 20 10 0 -10 -20 -30

3. Tuesday
Noon: 5°

Tuesday
Midnight: -20°

Change: ______

°C 30 20 10 0 -10 -20 -30

4. Wednesday
Noon: 15°

Wednesday
Midnight: 0°

Change: ______

°C 30 20 10 0 -10 -20 -30

During the next week, the Carters noted the daytime temperature and how it had changed by nighttime. What were the exact temperatures each night?

5. Friday Noon: -2°
It became colder by 6°.
Friday Midnight: ______

6. Sunday Noon: 14°
It became colder by 14°.
Sunday Midnight: ______

Name ______________________ Date ______________

Highs and Lows

DIRECTIONS

Study the graph of Bay Town's average temperature for 2 years. Think about the information the graph is giving you. Use the graph to answer the questions.

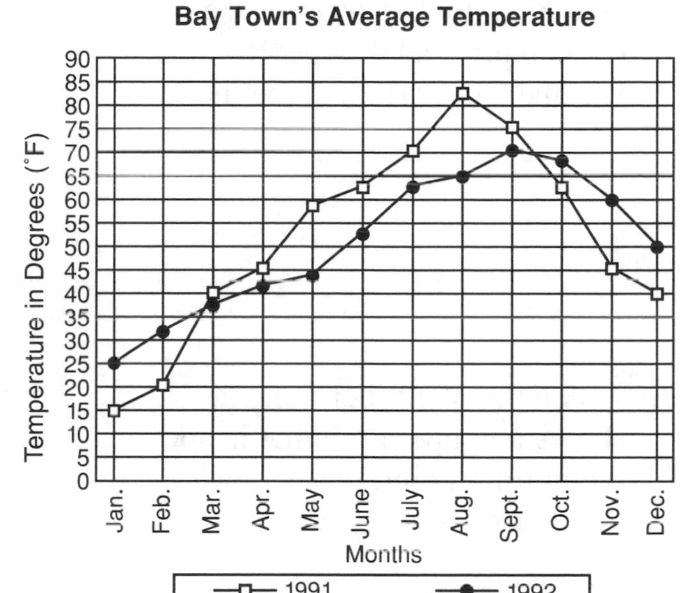

1. During which year were the average temperatures higher?

____

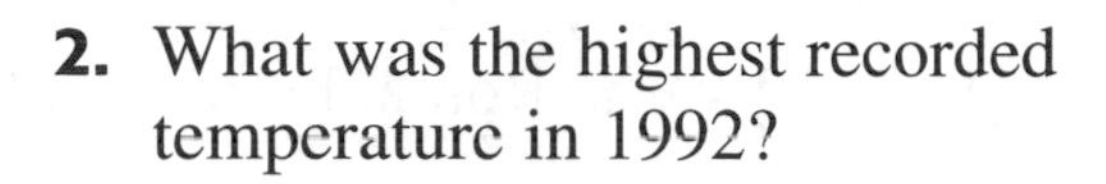

2. What was the highest recorded temperature in 1992?

____

3. What was the difference between the highest temperatures for both years?

____

4. Which year experienced the greatest decrease in temperature between 2 months?

____

5. How much did the temperature drop between those 2 months?

____

6. What was the difference between the average temperatures in January and August of 1991?

____

7. During which year was the greatest increase in temperature between 2 months?

____

8. During which year did the average temperatures repeat in different months?

____

Name ______________________ Date ______________

Don't Get Burned!

DIRECTIONS

Read each problem, and solve.

1. When Chelsea went to bed, the thermometer outside her window read 5° C. In the morning, the temperature had dropped 10°. What was the temperature in the morning?

____

2. Ron wants to finish painting his house before it snows, but he cannot paint if the temperature is freezing or lower. On Monday the temperature was 40° F, on Tuesday it was 36° F, on Wednesday it was 32° F, on Thursday it was 31° F, and on Friday it was 34° F. On which days was Ron able to paint?

____

3. A Fahrenheit thermometer shows a temperature that is above the boiling point, but below 214° F. What is the temperature?

____

4. On her way to school, Emily slipped on some ice and almost fell. When she got to school 5 minutes later, she checked the thermometer in her classroom. It said 10° C. Emily told her teacher there was something wrong with the thermometer. Was she correct? Why or why not?

____

5. On May 2, the high temperature for the day was 53° F. Over the next 5 days, the high temperature increased steadily by 3° F each day. What was the high temperature on May 7?

____

6. The thermometer at their house read 78° F, so the Sanchez family planned a day at the beach. When they reached the coast, however, the temperature was 9° cooler, so they did not go swimming. What was the temperature at the beach?

____

Name ______________________ Date ______________

Weather Watch

DIRECTIONS

Keep track of the temperature in your town for 1 week. At the same time each day, guess what you believe the outside temperature is. Check a thermometer to see what the temperature actually is. Then, listen to the radio to hear what your local meteorologist says the temperature is.

Using 3 different colors, plot a 3-line graph showing your estimates, your thermometer readings, and the meteorologist's report for the week. Include a color key and a title. Are your lines close?

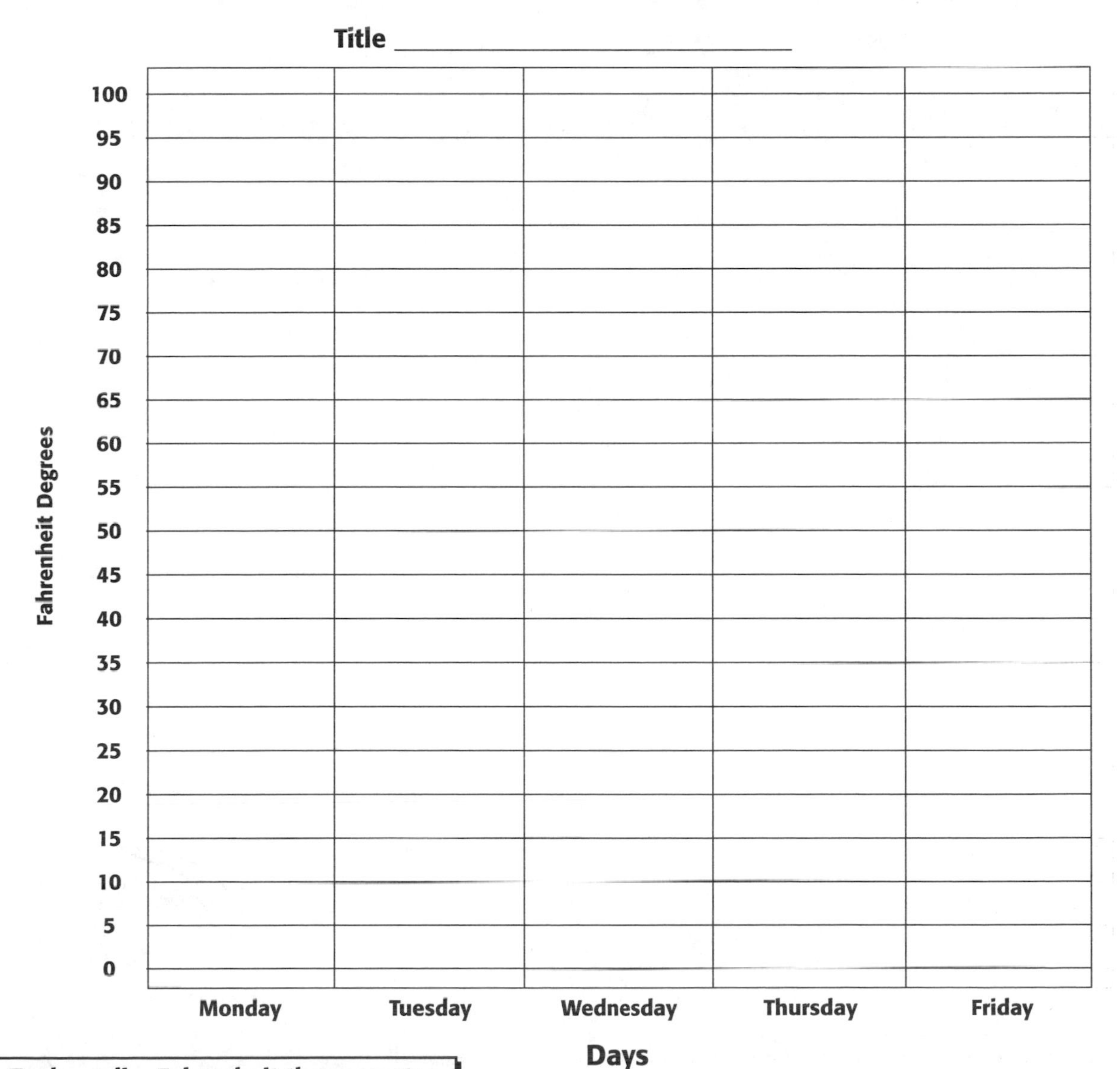

Tools: radio, Fahrenheit thermometer, colored pencils or markers

Name ______________________________ Date ______________

Worldwide Weather

DIRECTIONS

Use a globe to choose 2 places on Earth that you think would have very different temperatures throughout the year. Research the 2 places to find what the average temperatures are. What are the seasons like? How is the way of life in each place affected by the weather?

Record your temperature information in a 12-month graph using two colors. (Estimates for temperatures are OK.) Write 3 weather facts about each location. Draw a map to show the approximate location of each place.

Tools: globe, Internet or reference books, markers or colored pencils, ruler

Name ______________________ Date ____________

Unit 5 Assessment

Mass

DIRECTIONS

Read each problem, and solve. Darken the circle by the correct answer.

1. What would be the best unit to use to measure the weight of a horse?

Ⓐ ounces
Ⓑ pounds
Ⓒ tons

2. What would be the best unit to use to measure the weight of an apple?

Ⓐ grams
Ⓑ kilograms
Ⓒ milligrams

3. Which would be the best estimate of the weight of a car?

Ⓐ 1,750 ounces
Ⓑ 1,750 tons
Ⓒ 1,750 pounds

4. Which would be the best estimate of the weight of a can of beans?

Ⓐ 350 milligrams
Ⓑ 350 grams
Ⓒ 350 kilograms

5. Kendra's dog weighs 38 pounds. Her brother's dog weighs 23 pounds. How much heavier is Kendra's dog than her brother's dog?

Ⓐ 15 pounds
Ⓑ 17 pounds
Ⓒ 24 pounds

6. The school lunchroom uses 33 pounds of vegetables each day. About how many ounces does the school use each day?

Ⓐ about 500
Ⓑ about 700
Ⓒ about 300

Go on to the next page.

Name ______________________ Date ____________

Unit 5 Assessment

Mass, p. 2

DIRECTIONS

Read each problem and solve. Darken the circle by the correct answer.

7. Beth buys equal parts of 4 kinds of nails to make a deck. The total weight of the nails is 2 pounds. How many ounces of each kind of nail does Beth buy?

Ⓐ 4 ounces
Ⓑ 16 ounces
Ⓒ 8 ounces

8. Karen needs 1 kilogram of flour. She has 432 grams. How much more flour does Karen need?

Ⓐ 828 grams
Ⓑ 568 grams
Ⓒ 650 grams

9. Macintosh apples are 56 cents a pound. If Mrs. Dell buys 80 ounces of apples, how much will she pay for them in all?

Ⓐ $2.80
Ⓑ $3.00
Ⓒ $44.80

10. Each shelf in Adrien's bookcase can hold 63 pounds of books. Adrien has 175 pounds of books to put on the 3 shelves. Can the bookcase hold all of Adrien's books?

Ⓐ Yes, the bookcase can hold over 200 pounds of books.
Ⓑ Yes, the bookcase can hold 189 pounds of books.
Ⓒ No, the bookcase can only hold 126 pounds of books.

11. Cara weighs 95 pounds and 6 ounces with her cleats on. She weighs 94 pounds and 2 ounces without her cleats on. How much do Cara's cleats weigh?

Ⓐ 2 pounds and 1 ounce
Ⓑ 2 pounds and 4 ounces
Ⓒ 1 pound and 4 ounces

12. Tyler's dog weighs 10 kilograms. Three months ago, he weighed only $3\frac{1}{2}$ kilograms. How much weight has Tyler's dog gained?

Ⓐ $7\frac{1}{2}$ kilograms
Ⓑ 6 kilograms
Ⓒ $6\frac{1}{2}$ kilograms

Name ______________________ Date ____________

Weigh In

DIRECTIONS

Choose the most reasonable unit. Write oz, lb, or T.

1. a boy

______

2. a roll of tape

______

3. a bunch of grapes

4. an airplane

______

______

DIRECTIONS

Choose the more reasonable estimate of weight. Circle a or b.

5. 

a. 4 pounds

b. 4 ounces

6. 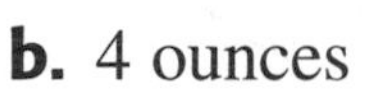

a. 113 tons

b. 113 pounds

DIRECTIONS

Complete each sentence.

7. 2,000 lb = ________ T

8. 32 oz = ________ lb

9. 3 T = ________ lb

10. 1 T = ________ oz

11. 500 lb = ________ T

12. 96 oz = ________ lb

DIRECTIONS

Write the number sentence, and solve this problem.

13. Mrs. Spence wants to divide $4\frac{1}{2}$ lb of peanuts evenly among her 12 students. How many ounces can she give to each student?

____

Go on to the next page.

Name ______________________ Date ______________

Weigh In, p. 2

DIRECTIONS

Choose the most reasonable unit. Write kg, g, or mg.

14. a computer

______

15. a dime

______

16. a calculator

______

17. a basket of apples

______

DIRECTIONS

Choose the more reasonable estimate of mass. Circle a or b.

18. 

a. 1 kg

b. 1 g

19. 

a. 8 kg

b. 8 g

DIRECTIONS

For exercises 20–23, write how many portions can be made.

20. 50-g portions of cereal

______

21. 15-g portions of raisins

______

22. 5-g portions of raisins

______

23. 75-mg portions of coconut

______

DIRECTIONS

Write the number sentence, and solve this problem.

24. Three blueberry muffins have a mass of 65 grams. What is the mass of 3 dozen blueberry muffins?

______

Name ______________________ Date ____________

What's the Difference?

You can use a balance scale to measure the difference between the weights of objects. If the weight on the left is 1 gram and the weight on the right is 4 grams, then the scale will read 3 grams.

DIRECTIONS

Use weights of 1 gram, 4 grams, 8 grams, and 16 grams to complete the table.

Left side	Scale reading	Right side
1 g	7 g	
8 g		16 g
4 g	12 g	
	4 g	4 g + 16 g
4 g + 4 g	0	
	3 g	1 g + 4 g
8 g +16 g	19 g	
	27 g	1 g
	5 g	16 g + 1 g
16 g + 4 g	7 g	
16 g	13 g	
	11 g	1 g + 8 g
	13 g	8 g
16 g	11 g	
28 g	1 g	

Name ______________________ Date ______________

They've Got Drive

Double-bar graphs are used to compare 2 sets of information that cover the same period of time. When the student councils at Pine Ridge School and Marble Creek School had a 4-week newspaper drive, they used a double-bar graph to show the number of pounds they collected each week.

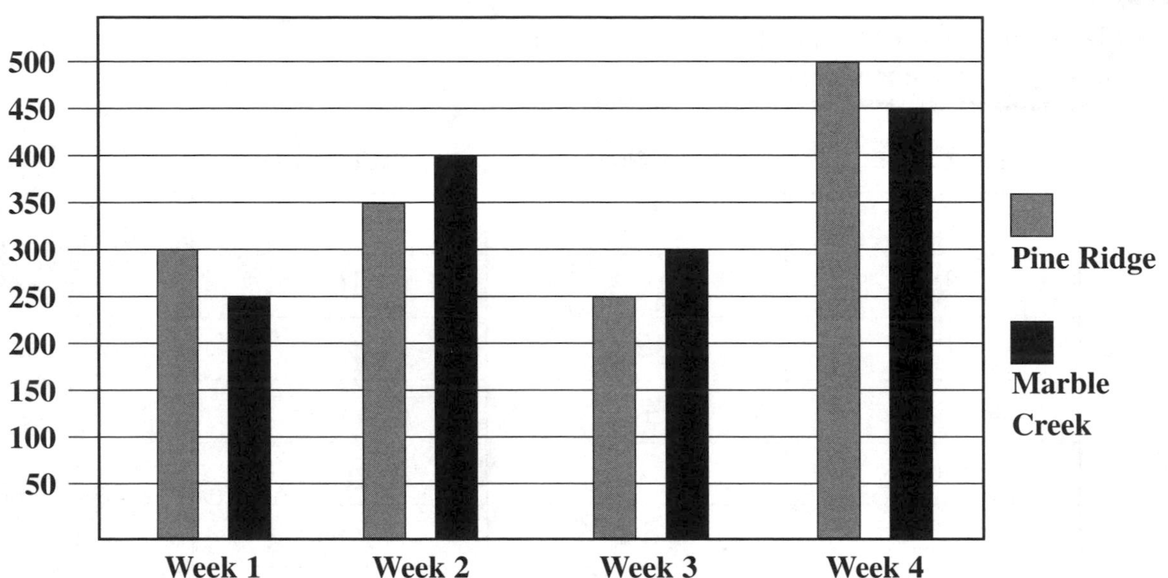

DIRECTIONS

Solve the problems by using the graph.

1. How many pounds of newspaper were collected by both groups in Week 1?

____

2. Which group collected more pounds of newspaper in Week 2?

____

3. Which group collected more pounds of newspaper in Week 3?

____

4. Which group collected more pounds of newspaper in Week 4?

____

5. In which week did the groups collect the most newspaper altogether?

____

6. How many pounds were collected by each group that week?

____

Name ______________________ Date ____________

Weighty Problems

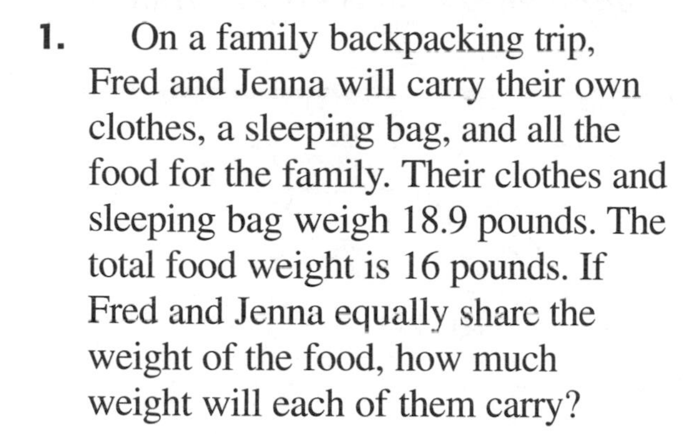

DIRECTIONS

Read each problem, and solve.

1. On a family backpacking trip, Fred and Jenna will carry their own clothes, a sleeping bag, and all the food for the family. Their clothes and sleeping bag weigh 18.9 pounds. The total food weight is 16 pounds. If Fred and Jenna equally share the weight of the food, how much weight will each of them carry?

____

2. Mrs. Lowe raises bees to produce honey. During the summer, 1 hive produces 108.75 pounds of honey. Another hive produces 95.4 pounds of honey. How much more honey does the first hive produce than the second?

____

3. When Mr. Rizzo makes pizza sauce, he uses 2 cans of tomato sauce that weigh 822 grams each and 1 can of tomato sauce that weighs 340 grams. He makes 16 pizzas from this recipe. How many grams of tomato sauce does he put on each pizza?

____

4. One of Mr. Rizzo's large pizzas weighs 5 pounds. The crust and sauce weigh 2 pounds 3 ounces. How much do the toppings weigh?

____

5. Apple pickers at Sweet Orchards picked 125 bushels of apples. Each bushel of apples weighed 60 pounds. How many tons of apples did they pick?

____

6. Sam and Ian went fishing. Sam caught a trout that weighed $3\frac{1}{2}$ pounds. Ian caught a trout that weighed $4\frac{1}{4}$ pounds. How many more ounces does Ian's trout weigh than Sam's?

____

7. You need 250 grams of cheese for a recipe. What fractional part of a kilogram do you need?

____

8. Marcie's mother baked muffins and breads for the holiday. She used $1\frac{1}{2}$ pounds of nuts for both recipes. If she used $\frac{3}{4}$ pound of nuts for the muffins, how much did she use for the breads?

____

Name ______________________ Date ______________

Ways to Weigh

DIRECTIONS

Without weights, how can you use a balance to weigh different items? List at least 3 ways, and experiment with each one. Which do you think is the best method? Why?

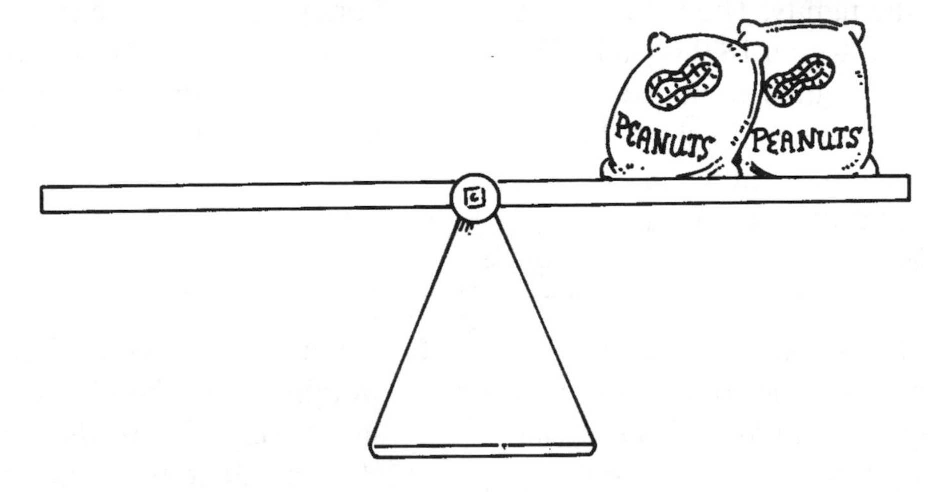

1. ______________________________
2. ______________________________
3. ______________________________

Best Method

____

____

____

Tools: balance, various objects to weigh, objects of known weight

Name ______________________ Date ____________

Unit 6 Assessment
Time

DIRECTIONS

Read each problem, and solve. Darken the circle by the correct answer. Use the graph to answer questions 1–4.

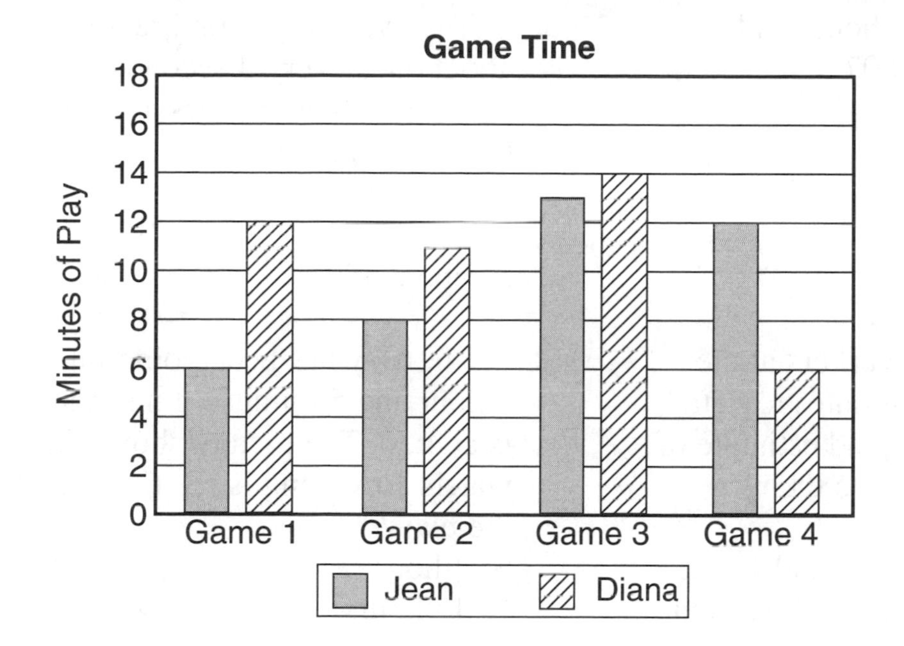

1. Who played longer during Game 4?
- Ⓐ Diana
- Ⓑ Jean
- Ⓒ They both played the same amount of time.

2. In all 4 games, how many minutes more did Diana play than Jean did?
- Ⓐ 5 minutes more
- Ⓑ 3 minutes more
- Ⓒ 4 minutes more

3. During which 2 games did the girls play exactly the opposite number of minutes?
- Ⓐ Game 1 and Game 3
- Ⓑ Game 1 and Game 4
- Ⓒ Game 3 and Game 4

4. If Diana continues to play the average number of minutes that she has been playing, about how many more games will she have to play in order to bring her total to 2 hours worth of play?
- Ⓐ about 11 more games
- Ⓑ about 16 more games
- Ⓒ about 7 more games

Go on to the next page.

Name ______________________________ Date ______________

Unit 6 Assessment

Time, p. 2

DIRECTIONS

Read each problem, and solve. Darken the circle by the correct answer.

5. What time is it 6 hours and 12 minutes after 10:07 A.M.?

Ⓐ 4:19 P.M.
Ⓑ 4:19 A.M.
Ⓒ 5:19 P.M.

6. The average person breathes about once every 4 seconds. About how many breaths does a person take in 2 minutes?

Ⓐ about 15
Ⓑ about 30
Ⓒ about 480

7. It usually takes workers at the Clean 'N Shine 8 minutes to detail one car. What is a good estimate of how long it would take them to detail 21 cars?

Ⓐ between 30 minutes and 1 hour
Ⓑ between 1 hour and 1 hour and 30 minutes
Ⓒ between 2 and a half hours and 3 hours

8. The play has been going on for 1 hour and 5 minutes. Intermission is at 4:30. The picture shows Jill's watch. How long is the first part of the play?

Ⓐ $\frac{1}{2}$ hour
Ⓑ $1\frac{1}{2}$ hours
Ⓒ $2\frac{1}{2}$ hours

9. What time will it be in 3 hours and 50 minutes?

Ⓐ 9:50
Ⓑ 10:10
Ⓒ 10:00

10. It is 10:45 A.M. now. Simon goes swimming in $2\frac{1}{2}$ hours. If he swims for 45 minutes, what time will it be when he is finished swimming?

Ⓐ 2:00 P.M.
Ⓑ 1:45 P.M.
Ⓒ 2:15 P.M.

Name ______________________ Date ______________

Watch the Clock

DIRECTIONS
Compute the time when each event began or ended.

1. Leslic arrived at school at 7:25 A.M. It takes Leslie 45 min to walk to school. At what time did she start walking?

____

2. Lunch is served at 12:30 P.M. It takes 52 min to prepare lunch. At what time did they start cooking?

____

3. Dinner is served at 6:00 P.M. It takes 17 min for Sam to eat dinner. At what time does he finish dinner?

____

4. A boat arrived on Tuesday at 6:15 A.M. The boat was on the ocean for 4 days, 2 hr, and 34 min. When did the boat set sail?

____

DIRECTIONS
Add or subtract.

5. 6 hr 21 min − 3 hr 53 min

6. 4 min 25 sec + 5 min 51 sec

7. 8 min 19 sec − 4 min 46 sec

8. 6 hr 20 min + 2 hr 43 min

9. 8 min 15 sec − 7 min 31 sec

10. 8 hr 0 min − 4 hr 34 min

DIRECTIONS
Solve this problem.

11. Kevin started his homework at 6:50 P.M. He took a 30-min break and finished his work at 9:15 P.M. How long did he work on his homework?

____

Name ______________________ Date ____________

Time to Figure

DIRECTIONS Complete each sentence.

1. 4 yr = ______ mo

2. 7 days = ______ hr

3. 108 mo = ______ yr

4. 10 min = ______ sec

5. 3 wk = ______ days

6. 2 yr = ______ days

7. 72 hr = ______ days

8. 6 hr = ______ min

9. 91 days = ______ wk

10. 210 hr = ______ days ______ hr

11. 3 hr 22 min = ______ min

12. 411 wk = ______ yr ______ wk

13. 511 days = ______ yr ______ days

14. 62 mo = ______ yr ______ mo

15. 1,024 sec = ______ min ______ sec

16. 2 yr = ______ hr

17. 3,648 sec = ______ hr ______ sec

18. 208 wk = ______ yr

19. 1 wk = ______ sec

DIRECTIONS Write the number sentence, and solve this problem.

20. Anita volunteers at the school library for 3 hours each day. How many hours does she volunteer in a 180-day school year?

____

Name ______________________________ Date ______________

Don't Be Late

DIRECTIONS

You plan to send a package from New York City to Bradenton, Florida. There is air freight service as far as Sarasota, Florida. From Sarasota to Bradenton, there is only bus service. All packages must arrive at the freight department of the New York City terminal 45 minutes before the flight. The ride from your home to the terminal takes 20 minutes. Use the schedule to answer the questions.

AIRLINE & BUS FREIGHT SCHEDULE—DAILY

Air	Depart New York	6:30 A.M.	10:00 A.M.	1:30 P.M.	5:00 P.M.
Freight	Arrive Sarasota	9:30 A.M.	1:00 P.M.	4:30 P.M.	8:00 P.M.
Bus	Depart Sarasota	10:30 A.M.	2:00 P.M.	5:30 P.M.	9:00 P.M.
Freight	Arrive Bradenton	11:30 A.M.	3:00 P.M.	6:30 P.M.	10:00 P.M.

1. To arrive at the airline terminal at 10:00 A.M., when should you leave your home? ______________________________

2. Your package must go out on the 1:30 P.M. flight. When should you get to the terminal? ______________________________

3. If you deliver the package to the airline freight department at 9:15 A.M., when will it reach Sarasota? When will it reach Bradenton? ______________

4. You deliver your package to the airline freight department at 5:30 P.M. When will it arrive in Bradenton? ______________________________

5. You want your package to arrive in Bradenton at 3:00 P.M. When must you leave your home? ______________________________

6. The flight is 25 minutes late arriving in Sarasota. Will your package still arrive in Bradenton on time? ______________________________

Name ______________________ Date ____________

Time to Think

DIRECTIONS

You must use logic to answer these questions. Read the clues; then, fill in the table below each set of clues.

One night:
Annie went to sleep at 10:00 P.M.
Jamal went to sleep 20 minutes before Annie.
Li went to sleep 40 minutes after Jamal.
David went to sleep 50 minutes after Enid.
Enid went to sleep 20 minutes before Fred.
Fred went to sleep 35 minutes after Annie.
Jorge went to sleep 30 minutes after everyone else.

The next morning:
Annie woke up 20 minutes after Jamal.
Jamal woke up 60 minutes before Li.
Li woke up 5 minutes after David.
David woke up 5 minutes before Enid.
Enid woke up 25 minutes before Fred.
Fred woke up 1 hour before Jorge.
Jorge woke up at 8:30 A.M.

1. Write the time each person went to sleep.

Name	Time
Annie	
Jamal	
Li	
David	
Enid	
Fred	
Jorge	

2. Write the time each person woke up.

Name	Time
Annie	
Jamal	
Li	
David	
Enid	
Fred	
Jorge	

DIRECTIONS

Use the completed tables to answer each question.

3. Who woke up at 8:00 A.M.? ____________

4. Who woke up at 7:00 A.M.? ____________

5. Who slept the shortest time? ____________

6. Who slept the longest time? ____________

7. Who went to bed at 10:15 P.M.? ____________

8. Who slept 8 hours 55 minutes? ____________

Name ______________________________ Date ______________

Across the Miles

TIME ZONES OF THE CONTIGUOUS UNITED STATES

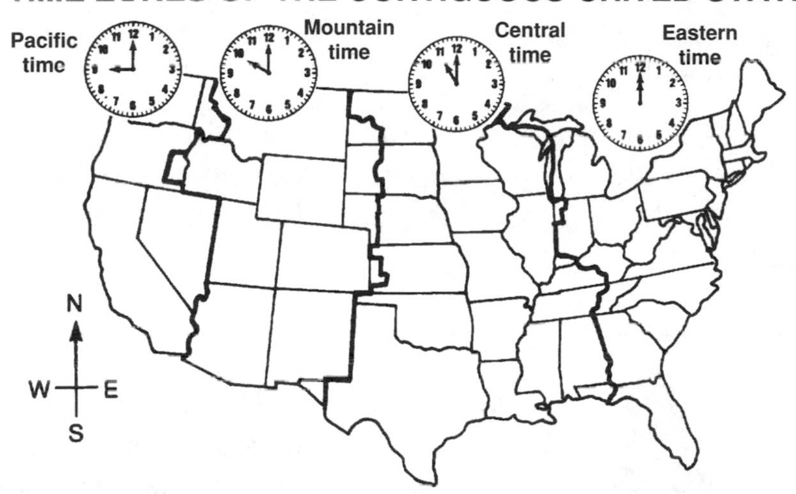

DIRECTIONS

Use the time-zone map to answer these questions.

1. Which time zone is this state in?

____

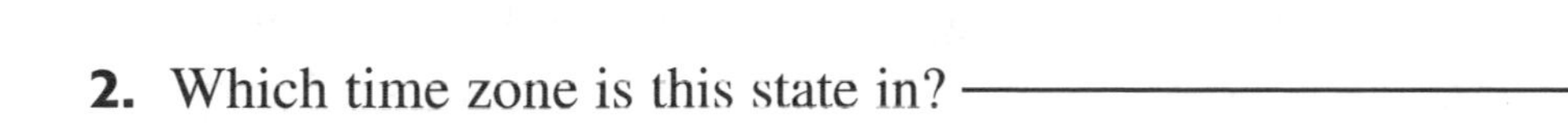

2. Which time zone is this state in?

____

3. If it is noon in this state, what time is it in most of this state?

____

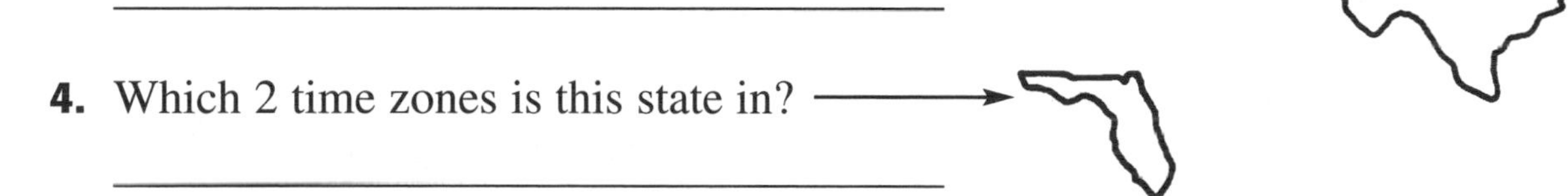

4. Which 2 time zones is this state in?

____

5. How many times would you have to change your watch if you traveled from this state to this one?

____

6. In what time zone is the only point in the United States where 4 states meet?

____

Name ______________________ Date ____________

Clock Talk

DIRECTIONS

Read each problem, and solve.

1. Chen's report will take $8\frac{1}{3}$ hours to complete. So far, he has worked for $\frac{3}{5}$ of that time doing research. How long has he worked?

____

2. Suki worked for $3\frac{3}{4}$ hours on her report on Monday and $6\frac{1}{2}$ hours on Tuesday. How many hours did she work in all?

____

3. If Sandy takes 15 minutes to give her oral report, what part of an hour does she use?

____

4. There are 21 students in the class. If each student takes 15 minutes to give his or her report, how many hours will it take for all of the students to give their reports?

____

5. If the reports are only given during 1 50-minute class each day, about how many school days will it take to get through all of the reports?

____

6. John spent 6 hours doing research on his subject. He spent twice as many hours doing research on the Internet as he did doing research in the library. How many hours did John spend in the library?

____

7. The students average 6 hours of research each. How many days of research did the students put in altogether?

____

8. The students spent an average of 9 hours each on their reports. If the students were given time to do $\frac{2}{3}$ of their work during the school day, how many hours did students have to spend, on average, working on their reports at home?

____

Name ______________________________ Date ______________

Reading Record

DIRECTIONS

A first-grade teacher asks your class to record some read-along story tapes for picture books. You get a 30-minute cassette tape. Which books will you choose to record? How many books can you read aloud on both sides of one tape? Be sure to include time for an introduction to each book and signals for turning the pages.

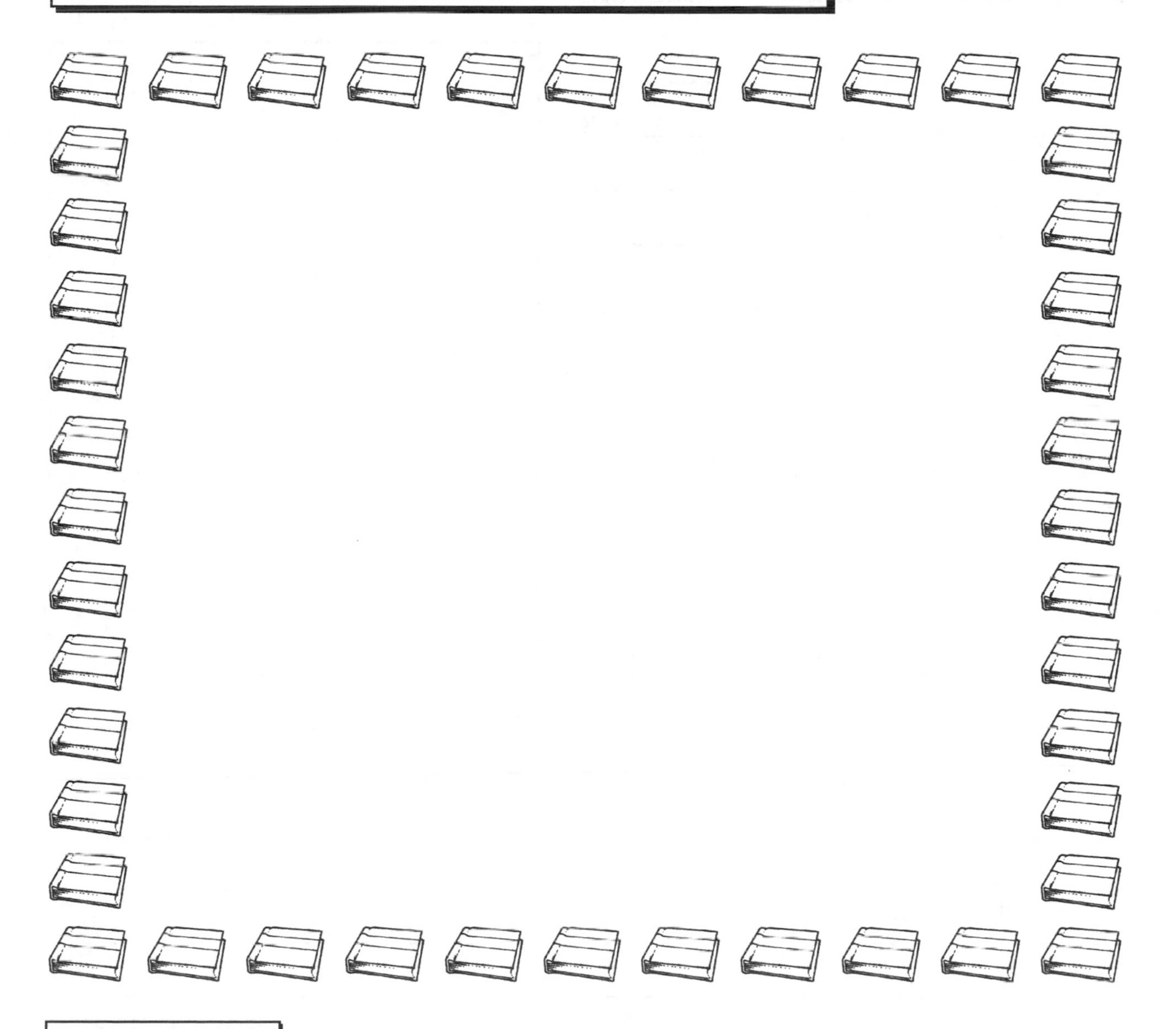

Tools: books, clock

Name ______________________ Date ______________

Kitchen Time

DIRECTIONS

Choose a favorite recipe. Plan how long it will take to prepare the food. Be sure to include the time it takes to get out the ingredients and to make the food. Draw a picture of the food you will make. If you can, have an adult help you prepare the food. Compare the actual time it takes to your planning time.

Name ______________________________ Date ______________

Unit 7 Assessment

Money

DIRECTIONS

Read each problem, and solve. Darken the circle by the correct answer.

1. Donald had 3 quarters, 4 dimes, 2 nickels, and 3 pennies in his pocket. He bought a candy bar for 63 cents. How much money does Donald have left in his pocket?

Ⓐ 35 cents
Ⓑ 65 cents
Ⓒ 26 cents

2. Jeannie has $1.73 cents on her desk. Which of these could NOT be the coins that are on Jeannie's desk?

Ⓐ 5 quarters, 2 nickels, 3 pennies
Ⓑ 2 half-dollars, 1 quarter, 4 dimes, 1 nickel, 3 pennies
Ⓒ 6 quarters, 4 nickels, 3 pennies

3. Jill had $6.35 in her purse. As she walked to the store, she found 2 quarters, a dime, and 6 pennies on the ground. How much money does Jill have now?

Ⓐ $6.76
Ⓑ $7.01
Ⓒ $6.99

4. Fiona wants to buy a stereo that costs $109.95, tax included. She has saved $55.49. She thinks she can save about $7.00 a week. In how many more weeks will Fiona have the money to buy the stereo?

Ⓐ 7 weeks
Ⓑ 6 weeks
Ⓒ 8 weeks

5. Alissa bought a set of paints for $7.84 and a new canvas for $5.99. If there is $0.05 tax on each dollar, how much did she spend on her purchases?

Ⓐ $14.52
Ⓑ $14.82
Ⓒ $13.83

6. Jonah bought a roll of film for $5.20, a photo album for $7.99, and batteries for $4.15. The tax was $0.86. If he paid with a $20 bill, how much change did Jonah get back?

Ⓐ $2.66
Ⓑ $1.80
Ⓒ $1.95

Go on to the next page.

Name ______________________________ Date ______________

Unit 7 Assessment

Money, p. 2

DIRECTIONS

Read each problem, and solve. Darken the circle by the correct answer.

7. Drew gets $3.00 an hour for baby-sitting 1 child, and $4.00 an hour for baby-sitting 2 children. She baby-sat for 26 hours in the month of July. Half of the time she watched 1 child, and the other half of the time she watched 2 children. How much money did she make?

Ⓐ $182.00
Ⓑ $70.00
Ⓒ $91.00

8. A movie ticket costs $7.25 for adults and $6.50 for children. The Smith family of 2 adults and 3 children go to a movie. Mrs. Smith pays for the tickets with a $100.00 bill. How much change does she receive?

Ⓐ $34.00
Ⓑ $64.50
Ⓒ $66.00

9. Sofia mowed the lawn 2 times in May, 3 times in June, and 5 times each month in July and August. She was paid $5.50 each time she mowed. How much money did Sofia earn altogether?

Ⓐ $55.00
Ⓑ $82.50
Ⓒ $25.00

10. Pedro bought some new clothes at a sale. He found a shirt for $6.98, socks for $1.29, and pants for $4.55. If tax was included in the price, about how much did Pedro spend altogether?

Ⓐ about $9.00
Ⓑ about $13.00
Ⓒ about $10.00

11. Jessie went to the store to get 1 gallon of milk, 3 pounds of string beans, and 1 pound of butter. She brought $6.00 with her. If the milk costs $3.15 a gallon, the beans $0.46 a pound, and the butter $1.23 a pound, does Jessie have enough money?

Ⓐ No, she needs $0.76 more.
Ⓑ Yes, she has $0.24 extra.
Ⓒ Yes, she has $1.16 extra.

12. Which of these means seven dollars and fifty-six cents?

Ⓐ $7.50
Ⓑ $75.06
Ⓒ $7.56

Name ______________________________ Date ______________

Cash Count

DIRECTIONS

Write the amount in dollars and cents for each set of coins and bills. Write the amount in words and in numbers.

	In Words	In Numbers
1. 	______________________________ ______________________________	__________
2.  	______________________________ ______________________________	__________
3.  	______________________________ ______________________________	__________
4. 	______________________________ ______________________________	__________
5. 	______________________________ ______________________________	__________

Name ______________________ Date ____________

Mind Over Money

DIRECTIONS

Read each problem. Use logic to answer the questions.

1. Kazuko has 1 dollar and 30 cents in nickels, dimes, and quarters. She has twice as many nickels as dimes and twice as many dimes as quarters. How many of each coin does she have?

____

2. Jeb has 5 dollars' worth of coins, but none of them are nickels or quarters. He has 1 half-dollar. He has a total of 100 coins. How many dimes and pennies does he have?

____

3. Nikki has 6 coins. She has some dimes, nickels, and pennies. She has at least 1 of each type of coin. She has more nickels than dimes and more dimes than pennies. What is the total value of her coins?

____

4. Huyla cannot make change for a half-dollar, a quarter, a dime, or a nickel. What is the greatest number of coins she can have, and what are they?

____

5. Ruth has twice as many dimes as nickels, and 5 times as many nickels as quarters. She has 3 dollars in coins in all. How many of each coin does she have?

____

6. Reggie has 2 dollars' worth of nickels, dimes, and quarters. He has a total of 20 coins. He has the same number of dimes as quarters. How many of each coin does he have?

____

7. Brad has $2.50 worth of 3 kinds of coins. The largest coins are worth less than the smallest ones, but their total value is twice as much as that of the smallest ones. The medium-sized coins have a total value of 2 of the largest coins. What are the coins, and how many of each are there?

____

Name ______________________________ Date ______________

Great Rates

Different countries use different kinds of money. The money that a country uses is called its *currency*. To buy things in other countries, you first have to exchange your currency for the currency of that country. The table shows how much foreign currency you might receive in exchange for 1 United States dollar. (Exchange rates often vary.)

Country	Name of Currency	Amount Received for $1 U.S.
Saudi Arabia	riyal	3.65
Spain	peseta	164.70
Egypt	pound	1.30

Country	Name of Currency	Amount Received for $1 U.S.
Greece	drachma	131.85
Mexico	peso	330.00
Norway	krone	8.24

You can find how much foreign currency you can exchange for U.S. dollars by multiplying. From the table, you see that $1 = 3.65 riyal. To find how many riyal you receive for $25:

25 x 3.65 = 91.25

You can find the amount of U.S. dollars you will receive in exchange for foreign currency by dividing. To find how many dollars you will receive for 57.68 krone:

57.68 ÷ 8.24 = 7

You must divide the larger amount by the smaller amount equal to $1 U.S.

DIRECTIONS

Read and solve questions 1 and 2. Then, complete the chart using the information in the tables above.

1. Bjorn thinks that 182.5 riyal is worth more in dollars than 7,411.5 pesetas. Is he right?

____

2. Lena exchanged 39.0 Egyptian pounds for Greek drachmas. How many drachmas did she receive?

____

Country	Mexico	Saudi Arabia	Egypt	Greece	Spain	Norway
Foreign currency			67.6 pounds		625.86 pesetas	
U.S. dollars	$55	$70		$69		$63

Name ______________________ Date __________

On the Money

DIRECTIONS

Read each problem, and solve.

1. At ABC Auto Supply, the cost of 6 flashlight batteries is $8.34. Smitty has only $3.00. How many batteries can he buy with his money? How much money will he have left?

____

2. At Purity, the price of trail food is $1.69 per package. At Supreme's, it costs $4.19 for 2 packages. Which store is offering a better deal? Why?

____

3. Mr. Salazar earns $9.35 per hour working in a camping equipment store. How much does he earn in 5 days, working 8 hours a day?

____

4. Maurice earns $12.00 an hour for cleaning a furniture store. When he works more than 8 hours in a day, he is paid for the extra time at 1.5 times his regular rate. If Maurice works 9.25 hours on Monday, 6 hours on Tuesday, and 8.75 hours on Wednesday, how much money does he earn for those 3 days?

____

5. Claire buys 1 pound of nails for $1.29 and 2 pounds of screws for $0.91. How much tax will Claire pay if sales tax is $0.05 on each dollar? How much will Claire pay altogether?

____

6. Christina went to a party dressed as a caterpillar, and she shared the prize for the funniest costume with Mark. Since no one dressed in a scary costume, the judges decided to combine the $10.00 for the scariest costume with the $15.00 prize for the funniest costume, and to divide it equally between Christina and Mark. How much money will each one receive?

____

Go on to the next page.

Name ______________________ Date ____________

On the Money, p. 2

DIRECTIONS

Read each problem, and solve.

7. Alfie and Marie are tied for the $25.00 prize for the most original costume. They give some of the money to Bobby, who helped them make the costumes, and divide the rest evenly. If they each keep $8.50, how much did they give Bobby?

____

8. The Jefferson School held a walkathon to raise money for their media center. The goal was to raise $700. The total amount raised was $847.56. By how much did they go over their goal?

____

9. Gloria pledged to walk 15 kilometers. She earned $1.10 per km for the first 10 kilometers that she walked. She earned $1.18 for each kilometer over 10 km that she walked. How much did she earn for meeting her pledge?

____

10. Sara is planning to give a party. She will invite 15 people. She figures that a cake will cost $16.00 and cheese, crackers, and punch will cost $14.00. How much will Sara spend for each guest?

____

11. Rudy bought 2 36-exposure rolls of film for $4.80 each. It cost him $12.00 to have both rolls of film developed. What was the average cost per picture?

____

12. Ramona and her roommate signed a 3-year lease for an apartment. Each of them will pay $320 a month for rent. How much money will Ramona have spent for rent by the time the lease is over?

____

Name ______________________ Date ____________

Guess and Check

DIRECTIONS

Choose a partner for this exercise. Sit facing each other, and stand a book between you and your partner. Using play money, arrange an amount in dollars and cents that is lower than $5.00 on your desk. Do not let your partner see the money. Tell your partner the total amount of money you have in front of you. Let your partner guess exactly which coins and bills you have. You may tell your partner which part of each guess is correct. Once your partner has guessed correctly, it is his or her turn to choose coins and bills and your turn to guess.

(Note: Keep track of your guesses by writing them in the space below.)

Tools: play money

Name ______________________ Date ______________

Lunch Time

DIRECTIONS

You have invited 3 friends to join you for a special lunch. What will you serve? How much will it cost to serve 4 people? Research the nutritional requirements for a balanced meal according to the Food Pyramid. Then, plan your meal and the cost below.

Name ______________________ Date ______________

Price a Pet

DIRECTIONS

You want to buy a pet. You have permission to buy one, but you must pay for it and all the equipment and supplies yourself. You must also pay for the care of the pet once you have it. How much will the pet and equipment cost? How much will pet care and food cost for one year?

Choose the pet you would like to have, and research to find what the costs would be. Include a picture or drawing of the animal.

Name ______________________ Date ______________

Unit 8 Assessment

Computation

DIRECTIONS

Read each problem, and solve. Darken the circle by the correct answer.

1. What is the perimeter of this figure?

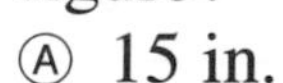

Ⓐ 15 in.
Ⓑ 20 in.
Ⓒ 20 ft

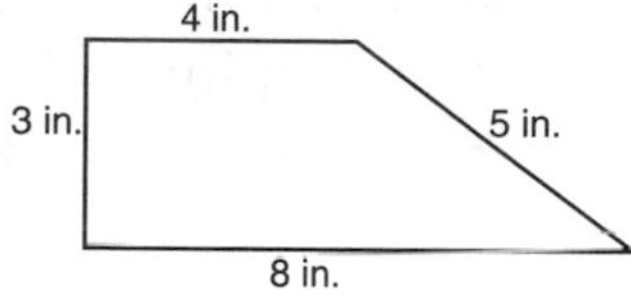

2. What is the perimeter of this figure?

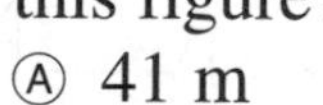

Ⓐ 41 m
Ⓑ 45 m
Ⓒ 55 m

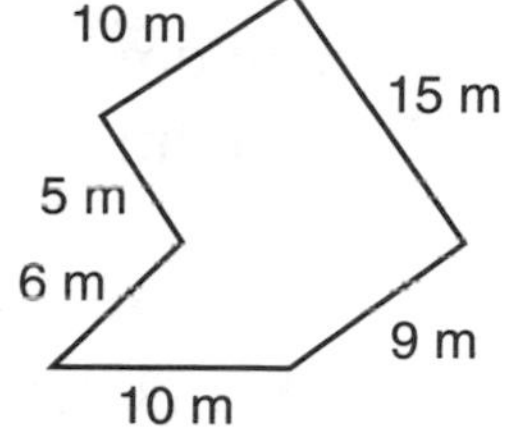

3. What is the circumference of this circle?

Ⓐ 28.26 in.
Ⓑ 18 in.
Ⓒ 28.35 in.

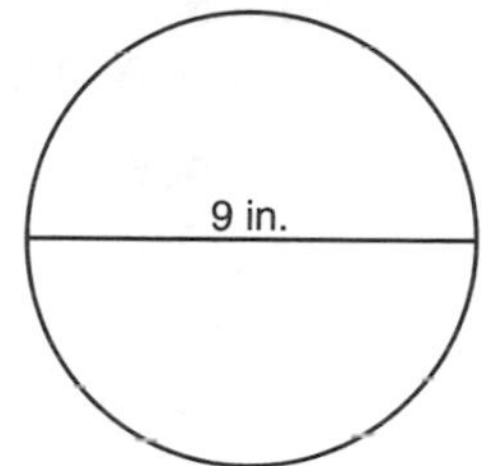

4. What is the area of this rectangle?

Ⓐ 120 sq m
Ⓑ 46 sq m
Ⓒ 130 sq m

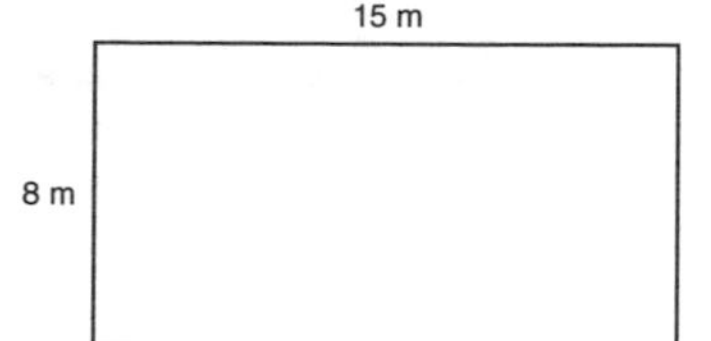

5. What is the area of this picture frame?

Ⓐ 92 sq in.
Ⓑ 504 sq in.
Ⓒ 450 sq in.

18 in.

28 in.

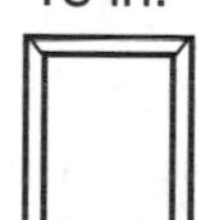

6. What is the area of this figure?

Ⓐ 40 sq in.
Ⓑ 24 sq in.
Ⓒ 28 sq in.

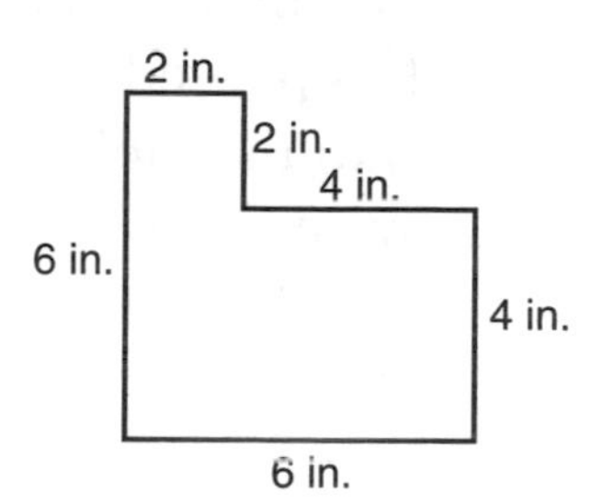

Go on to the next page.

Name ______________________ Date ____________

Unit 8 Assessment

Computation, p. 2

DIRECTIONS

Read each problem, and solve. Darken the circle by the correct answer.

7. What is the volume of this cube?

Ⓐ 8 cu cm
Ⓑ 6 cu cm
Ⓒ 4 cu cm

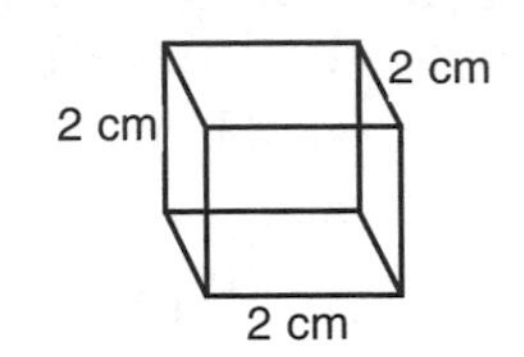

8. What is the volume of this box?

Ⓐ 17 cu in.
Ⓑ 52 cu in.
Ⓒ 160 cu in.

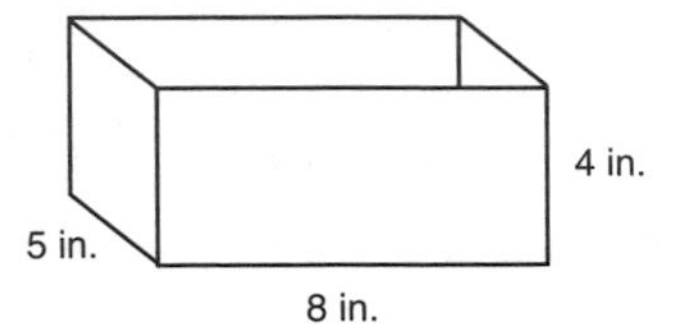

9. What is the volume of this aquarium?

Ⓐ 75 cu ft
Ⓑ 60 cu ft
Ⓒ 12 cu ft

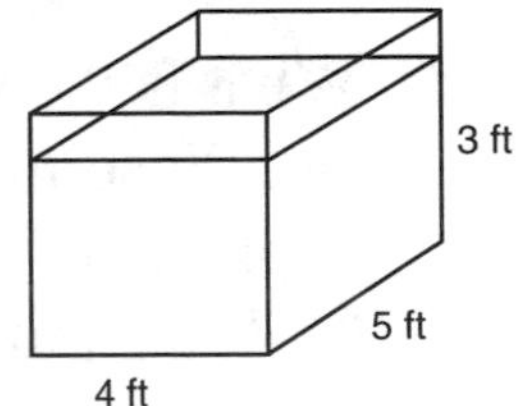

10. Jessica wants to put wallpaper border around the perimeter of her room. There are 6 walls that measure 10 ft, 12 ft, 15 ft, 8 ft, 5 ft, and 4 ft. How much wallpaper will she need?

Ⓐ 27 ft
Ⓑ 48 ft
Ⓒ 54 ft

11. Carlos' aquarium is 30 cm wide, 60 cm long, and 30 cm deep. He has poured 23,000 cu cm of water into the tank. How much more water will he need to fill the tank?

Ⓐ 24,000 cu cm
Ⓑ 31,000 cu cm
Ⓒ 15,000 cu cm

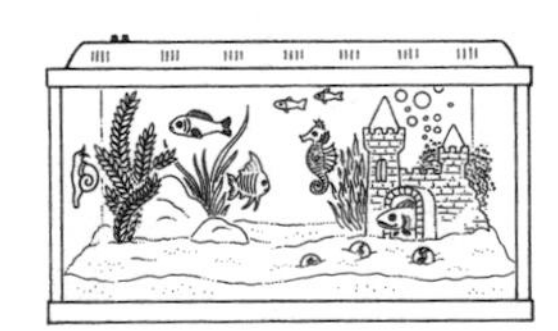

12. Mr. Morais wants to put grass seed on his backyard. His backyard is 13 meters wide and 26 meters long. How many square meters of ground does he need to cover with seeds?

Ⓐ 338 sq meters
Ⓑ 78 sq meters
Ⓒ 260 sq meters

Name ______________________ Date ____________

Perimeter Puzzle

DIRECTIONS

To find perimeter, add the lengths of all sides of a figure together. Find the perimeter of each figure.

1.

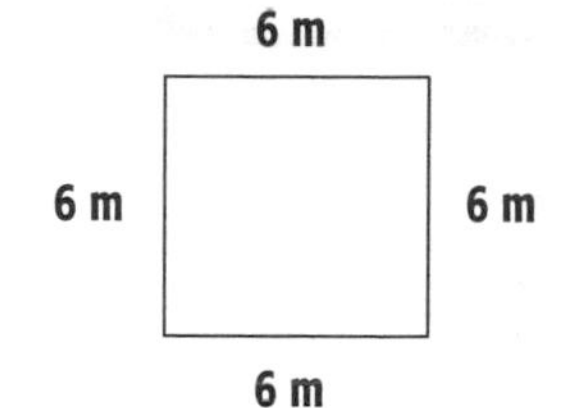

____

2.

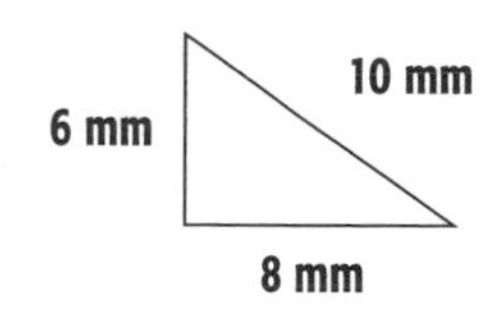

____

3.

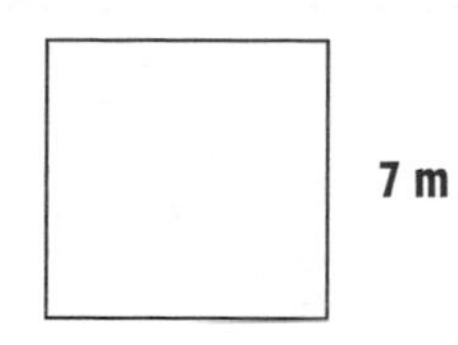

____

4.

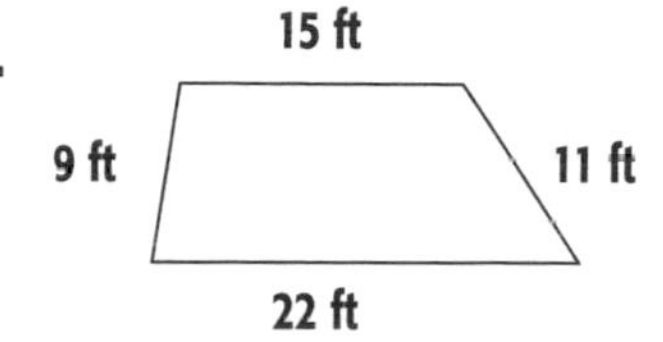

____

5.

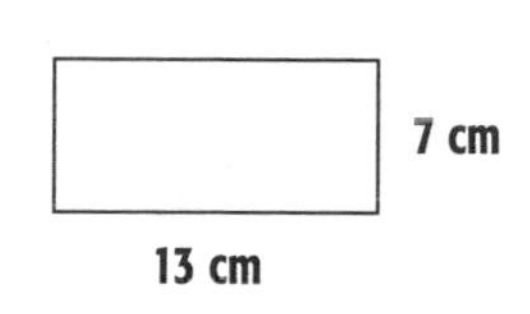

____

6.

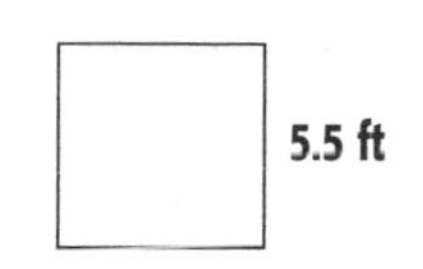

____

7.

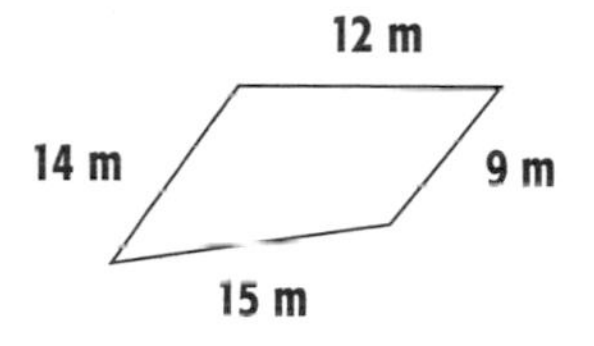

____

8.

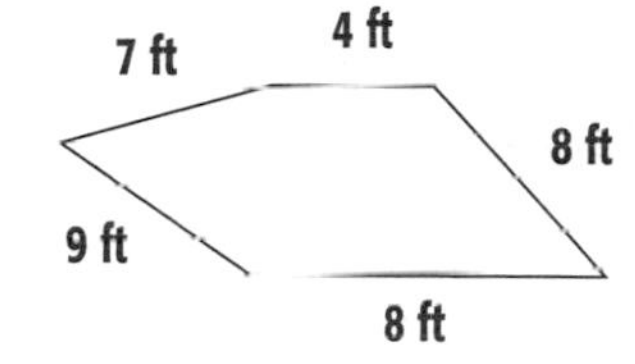

____

DIRECTIONS

Find the missing length in each figure.

9.

?

14 in.

Perimeter = 42 in.

____

10.

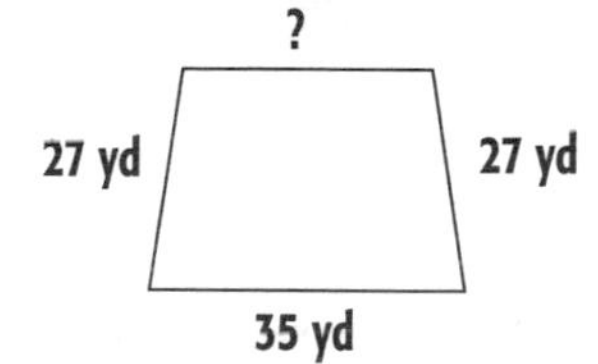

Perimeter = 119 yd

____

11.

Perimeter = 28 ft

____

DIRECTIONS

Solve this problem.

12. Steve is working on a jigsaw puzzle. When it is finished, he would like to frame it. If the puzzle measures 14 in. x 16 in., how many inches of frame will Steve need? ______________

Name ______________________ Date ____________

All the Way Around

DIRECTIONS

Circumference is the distance around a circle. Use this formula to find a circumference: $C = \pi d$ (π, or 3.14, $\times$ diameter) Find the circumference. Round to the nearest tenth.

1.

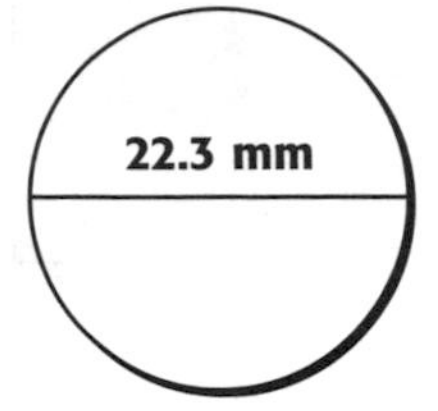

____

2.

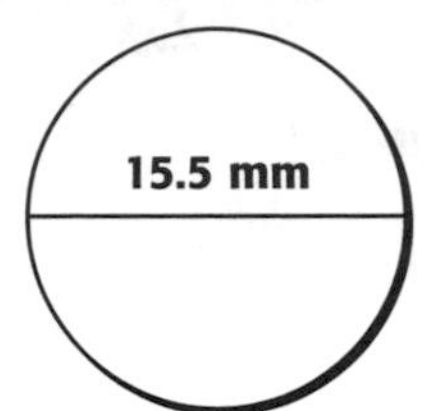

____

3.

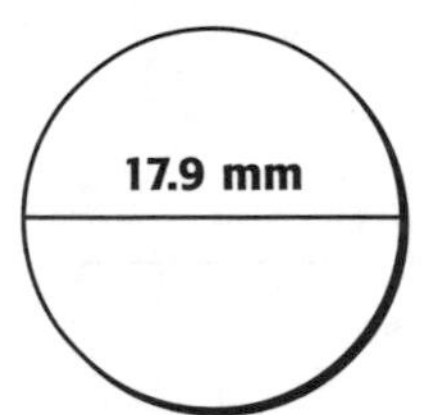

____

4.

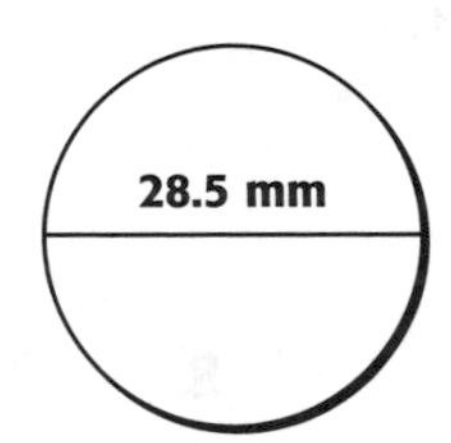

____

DIRECTIONS

Find the diameter. Round to the nearest tenth.

5. C = 84.5 cm ____________

6. C = 25.8 cm ____________

7. C = 189.6 cm ____________

DIRECTIONS

Find the circumference. Round to the nearest tenth.

8. 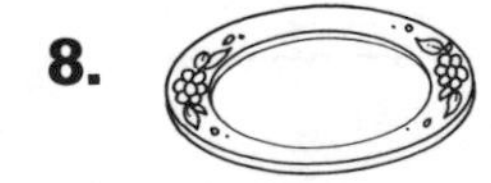 Diameter = 13.6 cm Circumference = ______________

9. 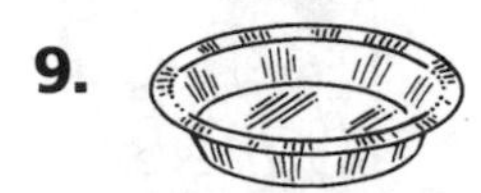 Diameter = 23.9 cm Circumference = ______________

Name ______________________ Date ______________

It's Plane to See

DIRECTIONS

Area is the number of square units inside a plane figure. To find the area of a rectangle, use this formula: $A = l \times w$, or Area = length × width. Find each area. Each square equals 1 cm^2.

1.

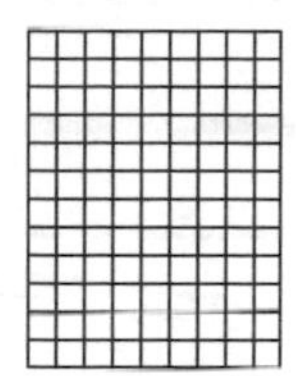

____

2.

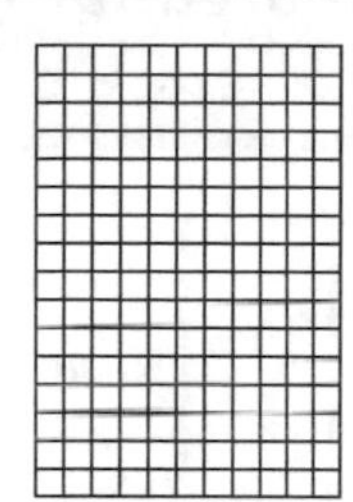

____

DIRECTIONS

Use the formula to find the area of each rectangle.

3.

4 in.

9 in.

____

4.

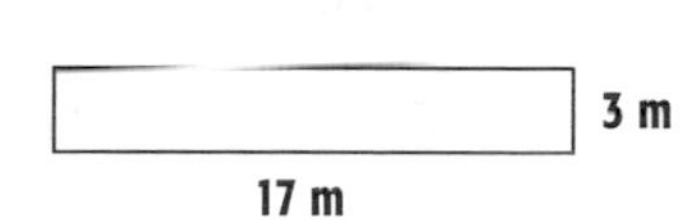

____

5.

6 in.

13 in.

____

DIRECTIONS

Measure each side to the nearest millimeter. Then, find the area.

6.

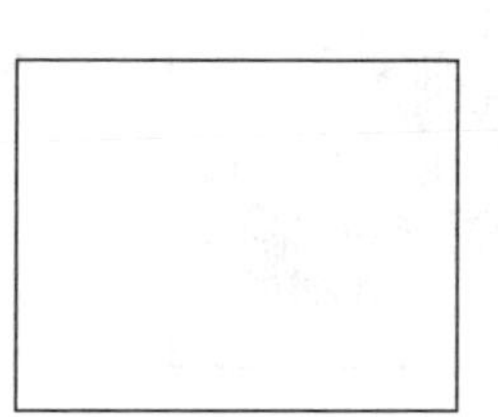

____

7.

____

8.

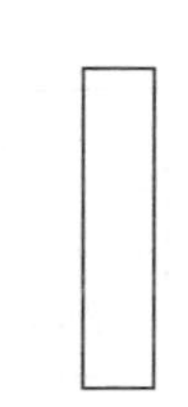

____

Tools: millimeter measure

Name ______________________ Date ____________

No Squares Here

DIRECTIONS

Area is the number of square units inside a plane figure. To find the area of a rectangle, use the formula: $A = l \times w$, or area = length × width. For polygons that have many sides, divide the figure into smaller, regular shapes. For curved figures, find the area for regular shapes. Then, estimate the remaining area. Find the area of each complex figure.

1.

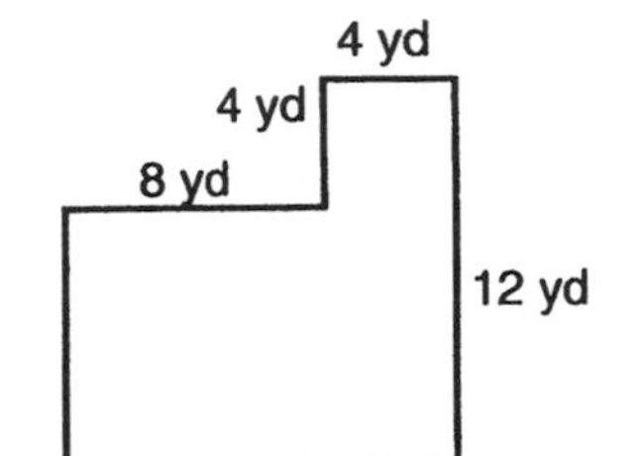

____

2.

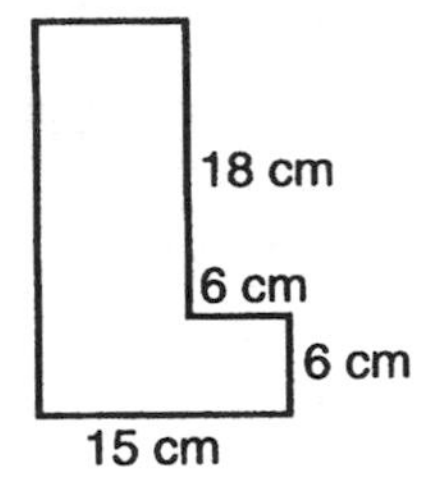

____

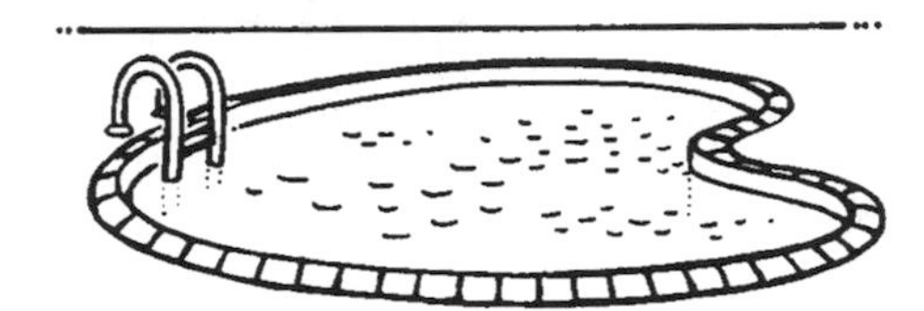

3.

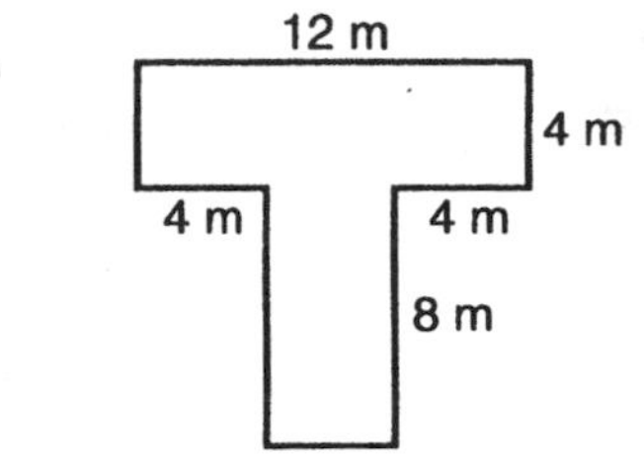

____

4.

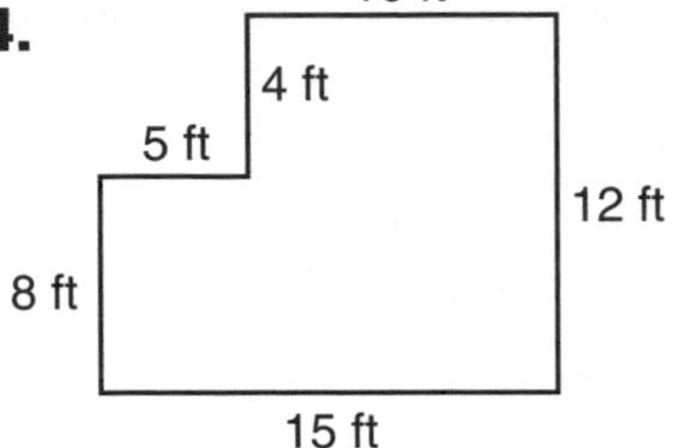

____

DIRECTIONS

Estimate the area of each curved figure. Each unit equals 1 mm^2.

5.

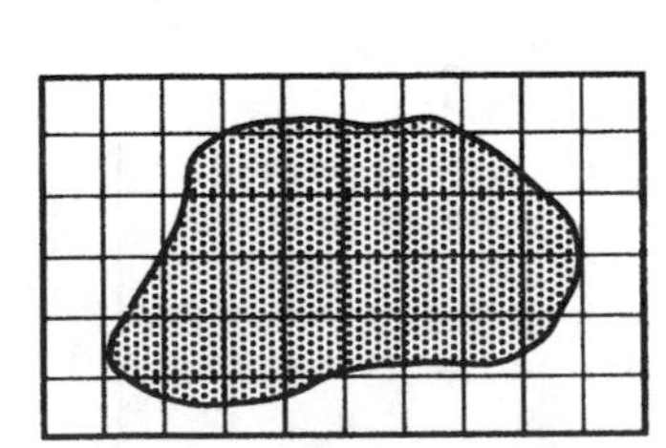

____

6.

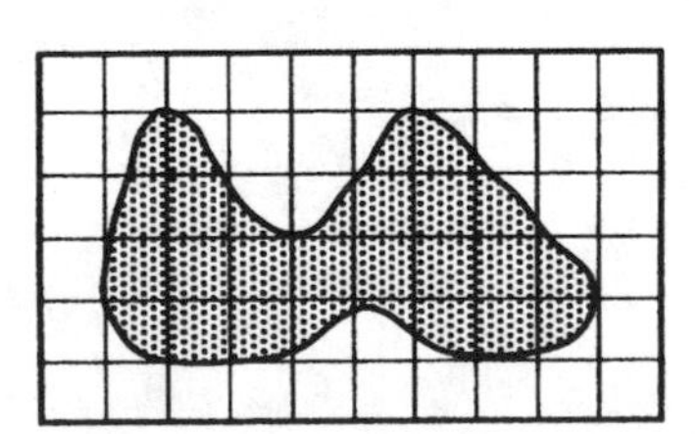

____

Name ______________________ Date ____________

Don't Let Area Scare Ya!

DIRECTIONS

To find the area of a parallelogram, use $A = b \times h$, or area = base × height. Use this formula to find the area of a triangle: $A = \frac{1}{2}bh$, or area = $\frac{1}{2}$ base × height. Find the area of each figure.

1.

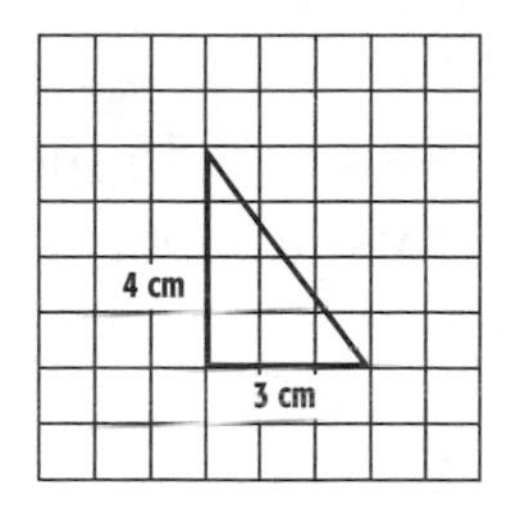

____

2.

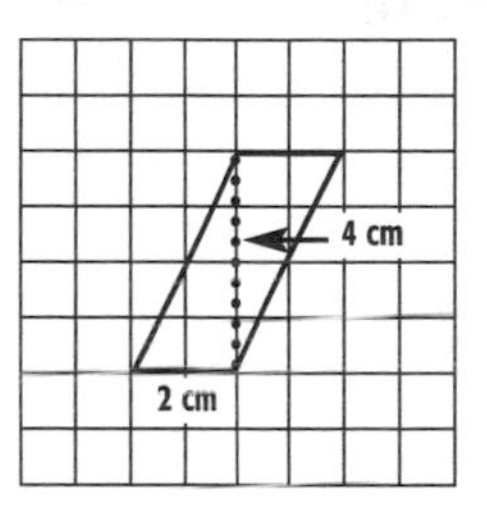

____

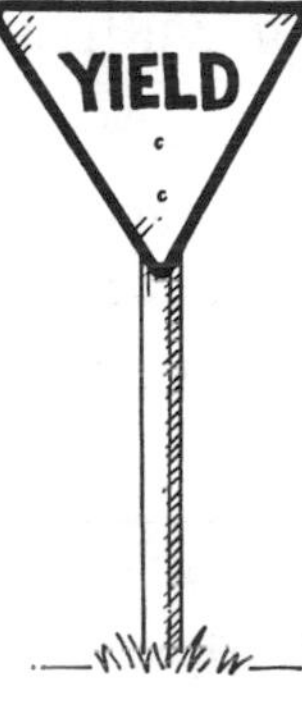

3.

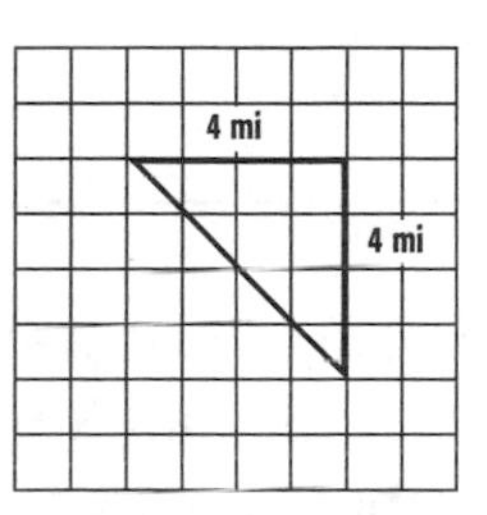

____

4.

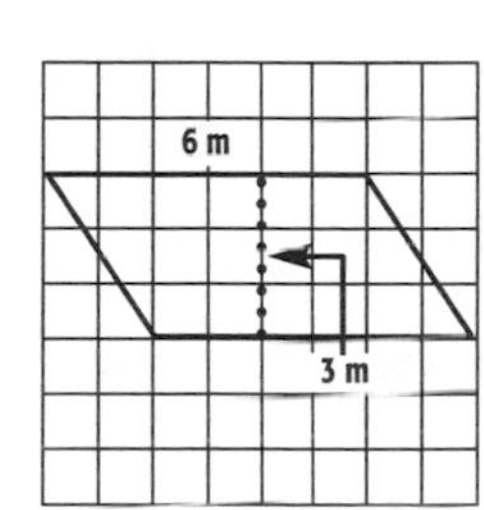

____

5.

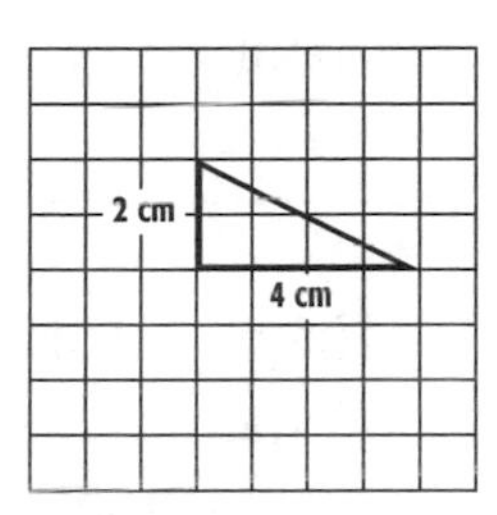

____

6. parallelogram
$b = 7$ in.
$h = 9$ in.

____

7. triangle
$b = 12$ m
$h = 8$ m

____

8. parallelogram
$b = 5$ ft
$h = 17$ ft

____

9. triangle
$b = 7$ft
$h = 4$ ft

____

10. parallelogram
$b = 3$ ft
$h = 7$ ft

____

11. triangle
$b = 9$ in.
$h = 8$ in.

____

Name ______________________ Date ______________

Homework

DIRECTIONS

Area is written in square units of measurement. To find the area of a rectangle, use the formula: $A = l \times w$, or area = length × width.

Janice is planning to wallpaper the rooms in her house. To buy the correct amount of wallpaper, she estimates the area of the walls in each room.

1. One wall in Janice's bedroom is 2.89 meters high. Round this number to its greatest place.

____

2. The same wall is 3.75 meters wide. Round this number to its greatest place.

____

3. Estimate the area in square meters of 1 wall in Janice's bedroom.

____

4. If all 4 bedroom walls have the same area, estimate the total area of the walls.

____

5. Each wall in Janice's study is 2.44 meters high and 3.05 meters wide. Estimate the area of the 4 walls in the study.

____

6. At the store, 1 roll of wallpaper is 0.75 meters wide and 8 meters long. This is about enough wallpaper to cover 1 wall in which room?

____

7. How many rolls of wallpaper does Janice need to cover the walls in the bedroom?

____

8. Two walls in Janice's living room are 3.84 meters wide, and the other 2 are 4.62 meters wide. If her living room is as high as her bedroom, estimate the area of her living-room walls.

____

9. How many rolls of wallpaper should Janice buy to cover her living-room walls?

____

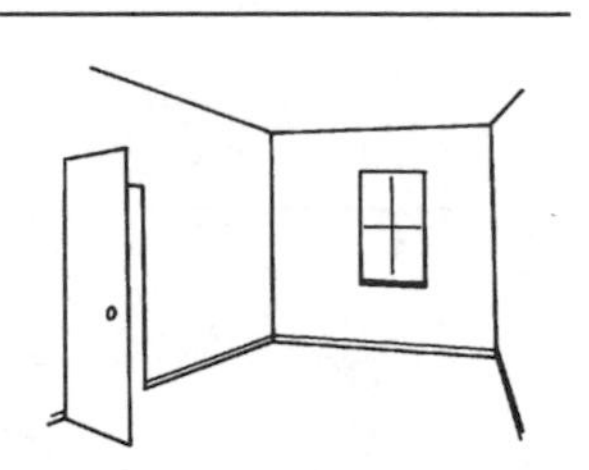

Name ______________________ Date ____________

Block by Block

DIRECTIONS

Use what you know about hidden cubes to find the number of cubes used to build each figure.

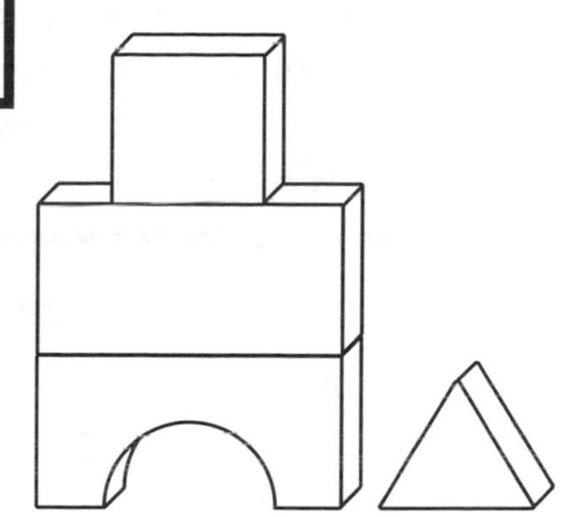

1.

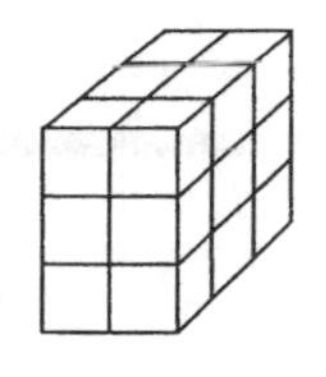

____

2.

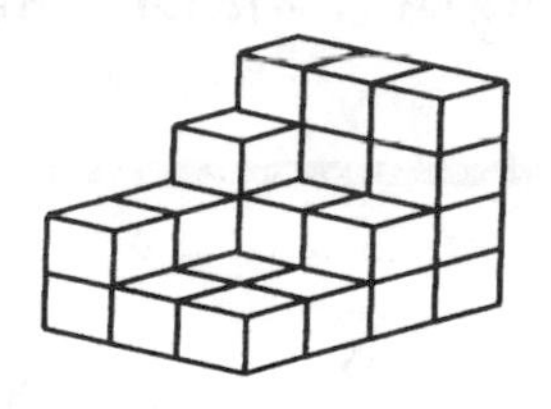

____

3.

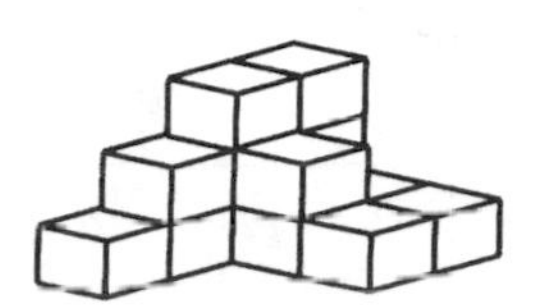

____

4.

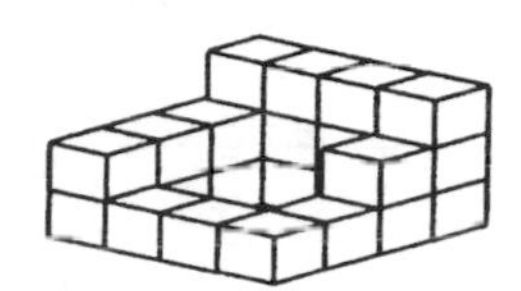

____

5.

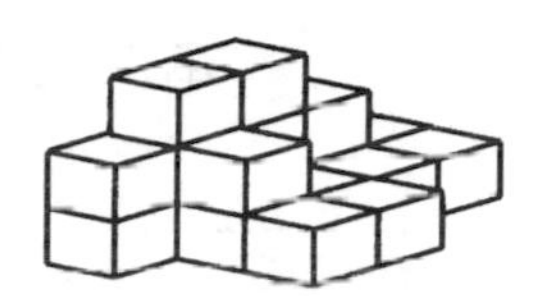

____

6.

____

7.

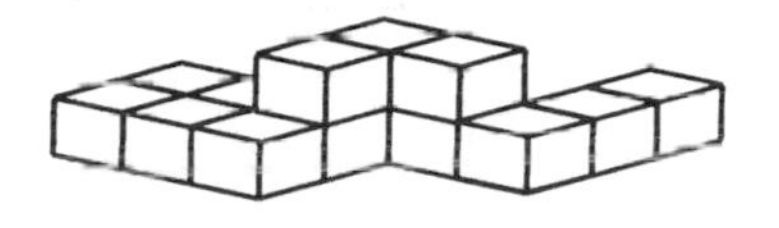

____

8. For which of the figures above is this the top view?

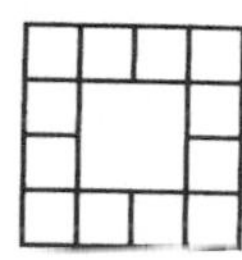

____

9. Name 3 figures above for which this is a side view.

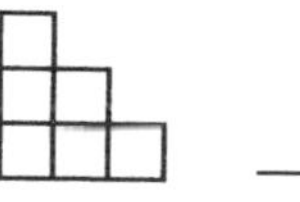

____

DIRECTIONS

Solve this problem.

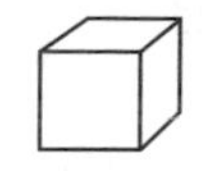

= 1 Cubic Unit

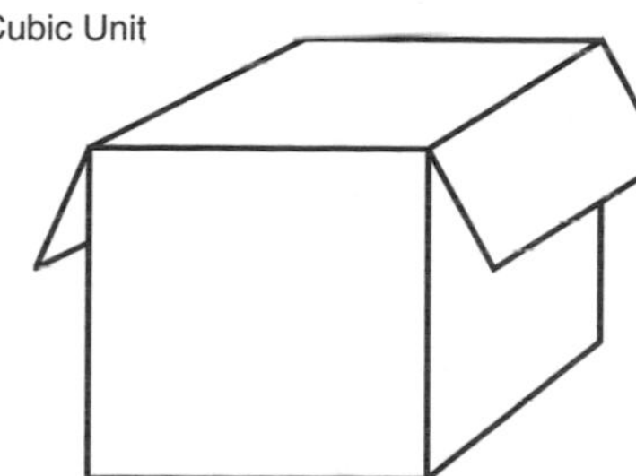

10. Mr. Kwong is putting math blocks back into boxes. He has 60 blocks left. Estimate the number of blocks that Mr. Kwong can put into the box. Will the 60 blocks fit?

____

Name ______________________________ Date ______________

Learning Volume

DIRECTIONS

Volume is the measurement of the inside of a three-dimensional figure. Volume is shown in cubic units. To find volume, use this formula: $V = l \times w \times h$, or volume = length × width × height. Find the volume of each prism in cm^3.

1.

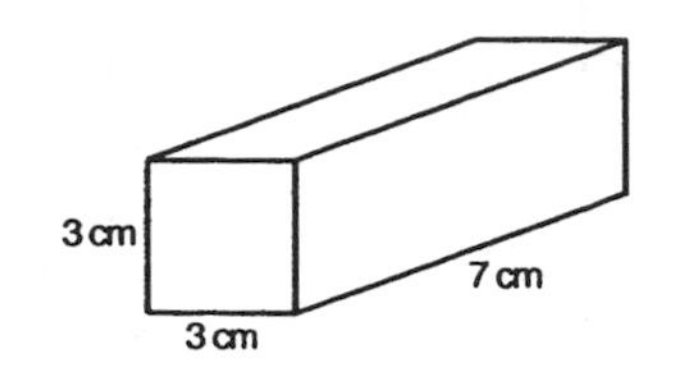

____

2.

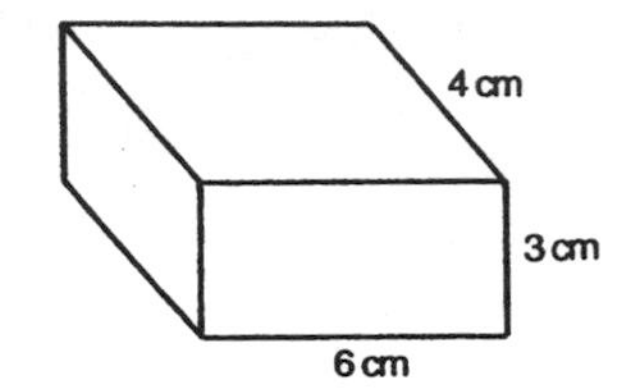

____

3.

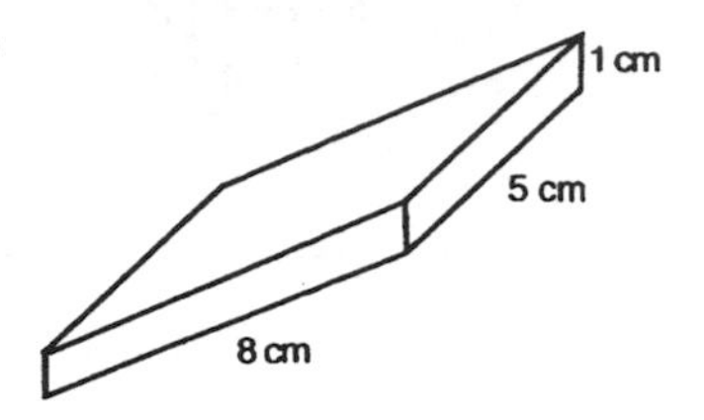

____

4.

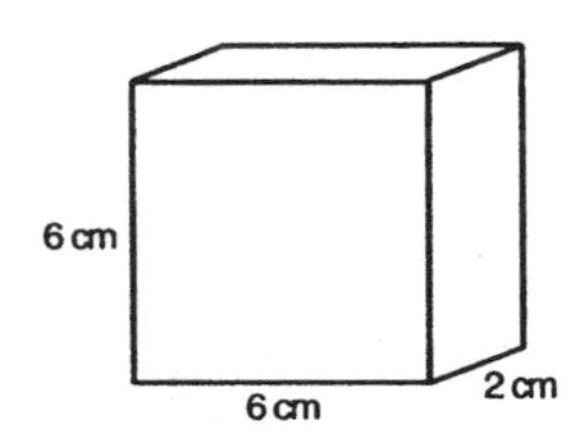

____

5.

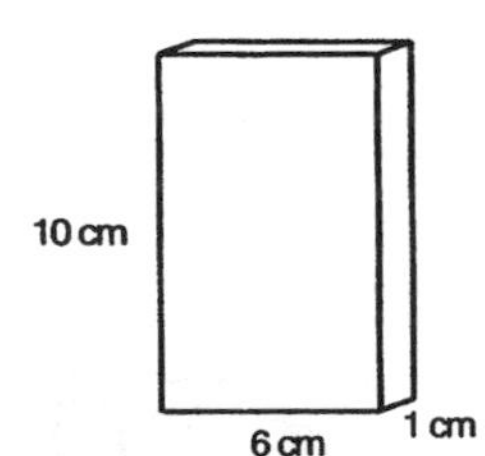

____

6.

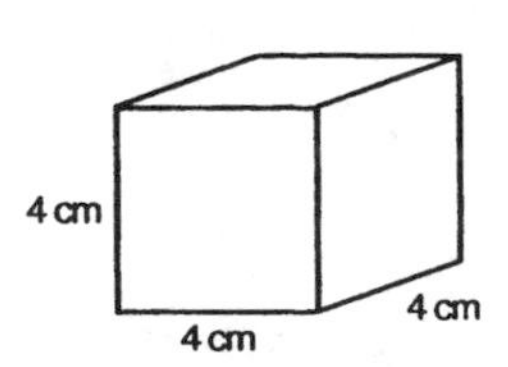

____

DIRECTIONS

Find the volume of each.

7.

75 ft × 25 ft × 8 ft

____

8.

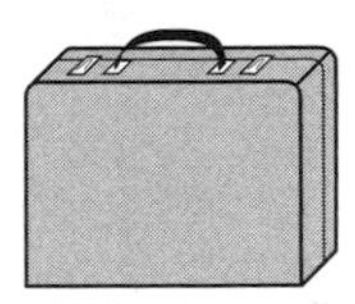

14 in. × 9 in. × 7 in.

____

9. $l = 7$ in.
$w = 8$ in.
$h = 5$ in.

____

10. $l = 20$ ft
$w = 10$ ft
$h = 5$ ft

____

11. $l = 50$ yd
$w = 25$ yd
$h = 10$ yd

____

Name ______________________ Date ____________

Break a Leg!

DIRECTIONS

Read each problem, and solve.

1. To make the background scenery for a play, a picture is painted on a roll of paper that measures 12 ft by 8 ft. The painter needs to build a frame around the back of it with wood so it will stand up. How many feet of wood does the painter need?

____

2. The smallest spotlight on stage has a diameter of 30 in. What is the circumference?

____

3. A toolbox on the stage is 20 inches long, 12 inches wide, and 10 inches high. What is the volume of the toolbox?

____

4. Jewel is designing a prop for the play. She draws a model first by drawing a circle on a piece of 1-cm graph paper. It covers 20 squares and 6 partial squares. Estimate the area of the circle.

____

5. The stage is a rectangle, 20 feet wide and 15 feet deep. What is the area of the stage floor? What is the perimeter?

____

6. The prop room is 10 feet deep by 8 feet wide. The trees that were made for props each take up 1 square foot of space. If $\frac{1}{4}$ of the prop room floor is available for storing the trees, how many trees can be stored in the room?

____

Name ______________________ Date ______________

House Map

DIRECTIONS

A floor plan is a map that shows the outline of a house. It shows the shapes of the rooms and where the doors and windows are located. What would the floor plan of your dream house look like? You must include areas for preparing food, for eating, for sleeping, and for playing. Add walls, windows, doors, and furniture. Show the dimensions of each room.

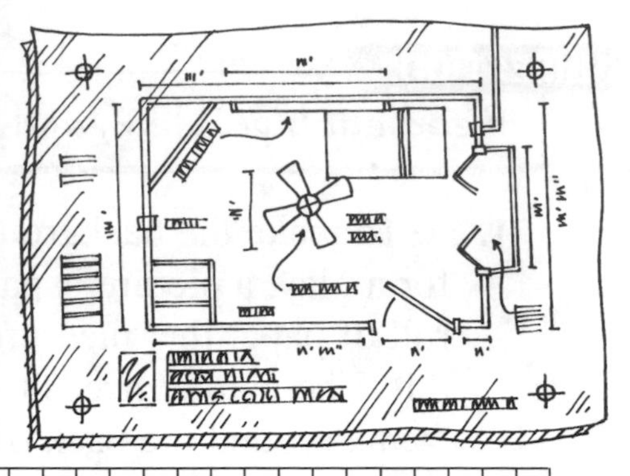

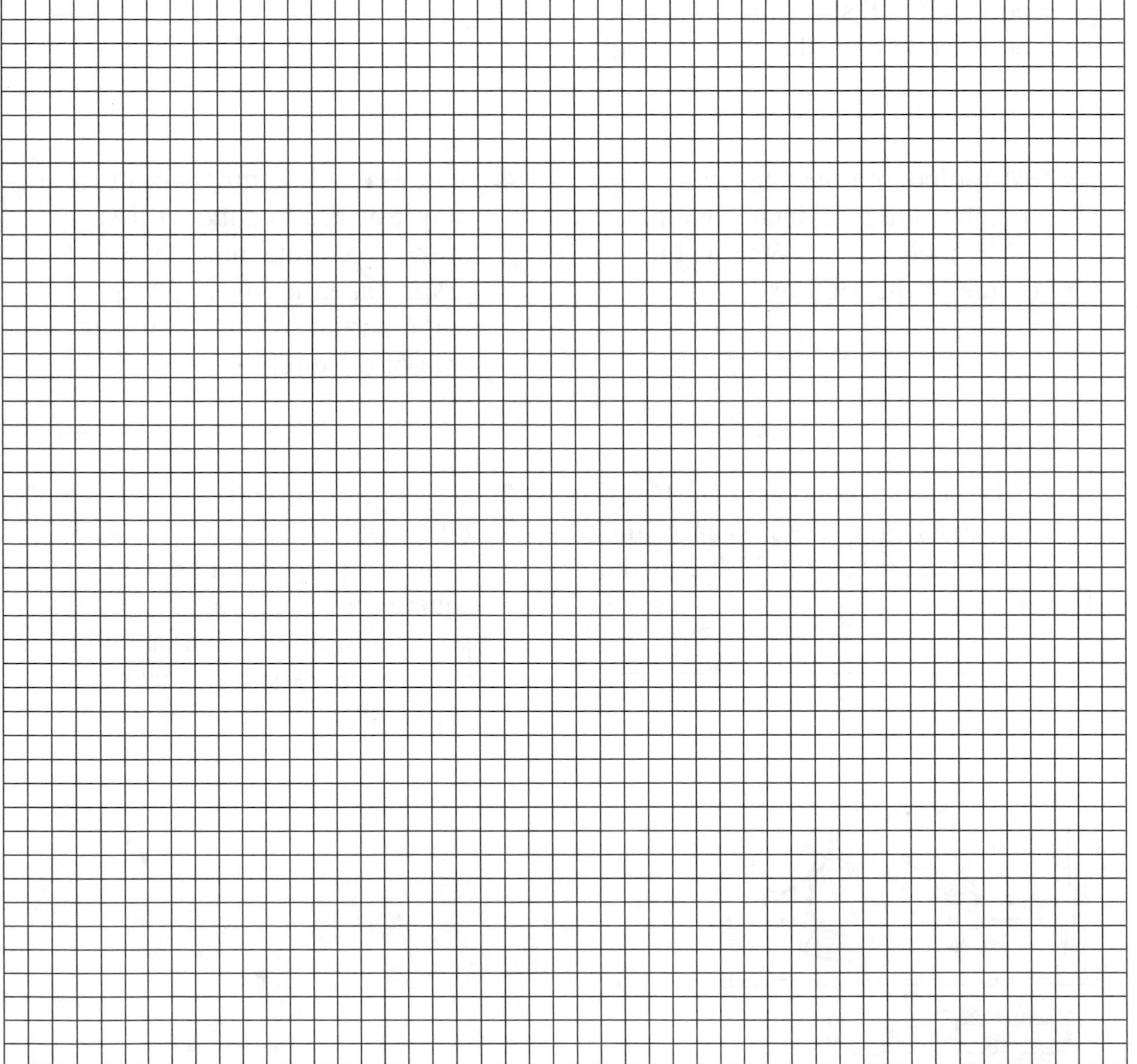

Tools: ruler, blue pencil

Name ______________________ Date ______________

Be a Sport

DIRECTIONS

What is your favorite sport in which a ball is used? Research the dimensions of the field, course, or court. Make a scale drawing of it. Show the dimensions in your drawing.

Tools: reference books, ruler

Name ______________________ Date ______________

Home Sweet Space

DIRECTIONS

Design and draw the interior of the space station below. Include areas in which 7 people could eat, sleep, work, and relax. How much space should you use for each area? What other kinds of areas might you need for a long space voyage? Use colored pencils to show different areas, and include the approximate size of each area.

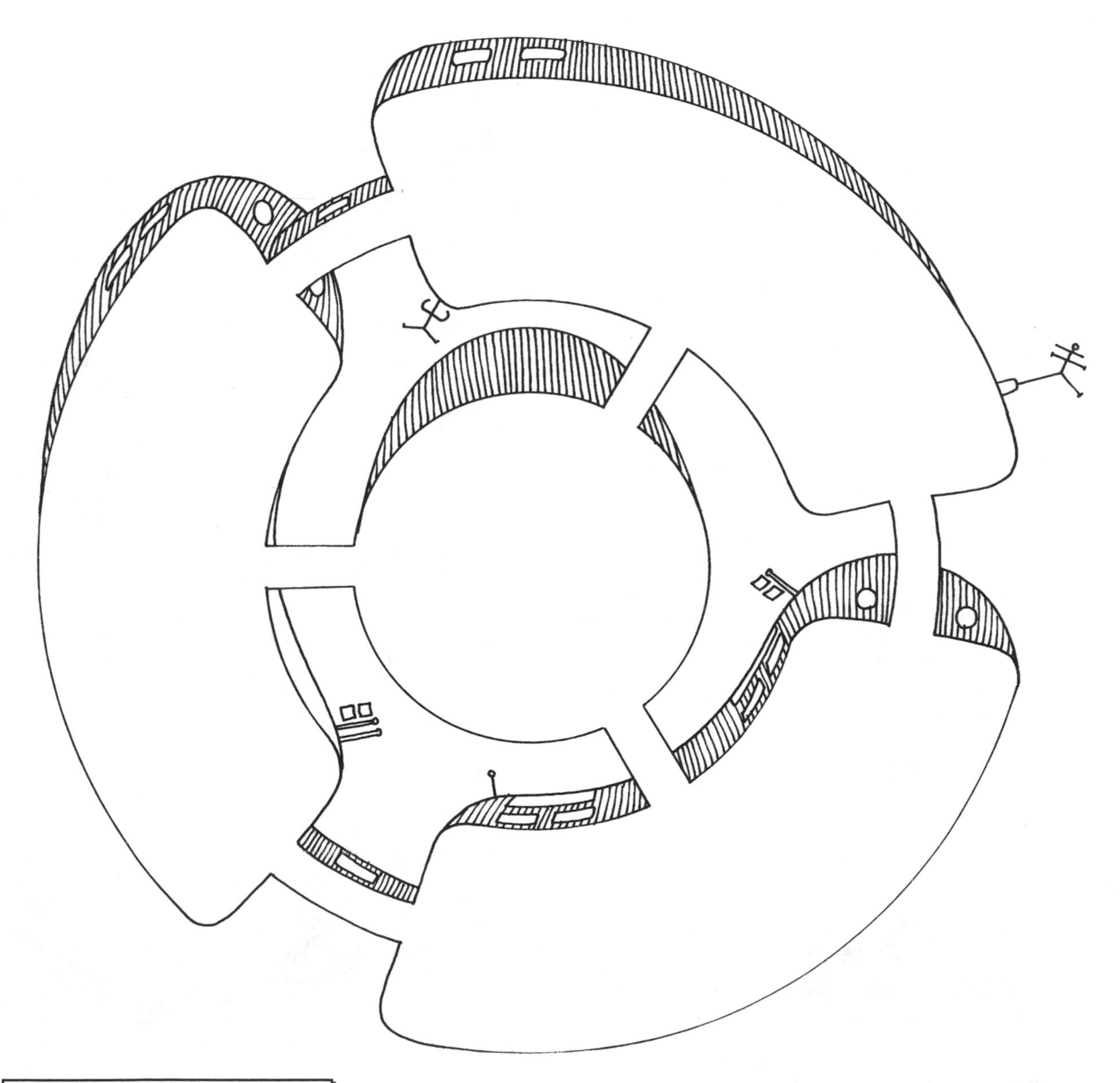

Tools: ruler, colored pencils

Measurement: Grade 5

Answer Key

Pp. 9–12
Overall Assessment

1. C	**17.** A		
2. A	**18.** B		
3. A	**19.** C		
4. A	**20.** B		
5. A	**21.** A		
6. B	**22.** B		
7. C	**23.** A		
8. C	**24.** C		
9. B	**25.** B		
10. A	**26.** A		
11. C	**27.** B		
12. B	**28.** B		
13. C	**29.** A		
14. A	**30.** A		
15. B	**31.** A		
16. C			

Pp. 13–14
Unit I Assessment

1. A **7.** B
2. C **8.** B
3. A **9.** C
4. A **10.** A
5. A **11.** B
6. C **12.** C

P. 15 Answers will vary. Check students' graphs for reasonable data.

P. 16 Answers will vary. Check students' charts for reasonable data.

P. 17 Answers will vary. Check students' graphs for reasonable data.

P. 18 Answers will vary. Check students' charts for reasonable data and correct calculations of differences.

P. 19

Dish	Estimated cooking time	Starting time	Estimated serving time
Soup	10 min.	4:50 P.M.	5:00 P.M.
Beef	2 hr., 45 min.	2:25 P.M.	5:10 P.M.
Potatoes	55 min.	4:15 P.M.	5:10 P.M.
Beans	15 min.	4:55 P.M.	5:10 P.M.
Dessert	65 min.	4:40 P.M.	5:45 P.M.

P. 20
1. yes
2. one more roll
3. no
4. Ward Hardware
5. 4
6. no

P. 21 Answers will vary. Check students' charts for reasonable data.

P. 22
1. C **4.** C
2. C **5.** C
3. B **6.** A

Pp. 23–24
Unit 2 Assessment
1. C **7.** A
2. B **8.** C
3. B **9.** B
4. B **10.** A
5. A **11.** B
6. C **12.** B

Pp. 25
G shows 4 5/8.
A. 1/4 inch
B. 1 3/16 inches
C. 1 3/4 inches
D. 3 1/8 inches
E. 4 15/16 inches
F. 5 1/2 inches
1. 1 13/16 inches
2. 1 11/16 inches
3. 1 15/16 inches

Pp. 26–27
1. miles
2. feet
3. inches
4. feet
5. miles
6. inches
7. feet or yards
8. inches
9. feet or yards
10. miles or feet or yards
11. yards or feet
12. feet
13. feet or yards
14. feet or yards
15. miles
16. inches
17. miles
18. feet or yards
19. inches
20. feet
21. kilometers
22. millimeters
23. meters or centimeters
24. kilometers or meters
25. meters
26. meters
27. millimeters
28. centimeters (or decimeters)
29. centimeters
30. decimeters
31. meters
32. kilometers or meters
33. kilometers
34. meters
35. millimeters
36. centimeters
37. meters
38. kilometers
39. centimeters
40. centimeters

Pp. 28–29
1. 2 3/8 in. **3.** 4 1/2 in.
2. 1 3/4 in. **4.** 2 1/16 in.
5–8. Check students' work.
9. 24 **14.** 4
10. 2,640 **15.** 3
11. 150 **16.** 3
12. 2 **17.** 3
13. 880
18. Bayard is taller.
5 3/4 - 5 9/16 = 3/16 in.
19. 4 1/2 cm
20. 1 dm (10 cm)
21. 7 cm, 3 mm
22. 7 mm
23–26. Check students' work.
27. 1 **32.** 1/2
28. 10 **33.** 1,000
29. 100 **34.** 1/100
30. 2 **35.** 1
31. 100
36. It grew 23.2 cm.
6 + 4.3 + 5.1 + 7.8 = 23.2 cm

P. 30
1. 1 1/2 miles
2. 4 1/2 miles
3. 6 1/4 miles
4. Rocky Flats and Oakmont; 6 1/2 miles
5. 75 miles
6. 237 1/2 miles
7. 87 1/2 miles
8. 225 miles

P. 31
1. 19 miles
2. 3 feet
3. 7,752 miles
4. 73.4 kilometers
5. 109,737 miles
6. 5 leaves
7. 11 1/4 spools

P. 32 Answers will vary. Check students' work.

Pp. 33–34
Unit 3 Assessment
1. B **7.** B
2. B **8.** A
3. C **9.** B
4. A **10.** B
5. C **11.** C
6. B **12.** A

Pp. 35–36
1. a **16.** a
2. a **17.** b
3. a **18.** a
4. b **19.** b
5. gal **20.** L
6. qt **21.** mL
7. tsp **22.** L
8. gal **23.** L
9. c **24.** mL
10. tsp **25.** L
11. 4 **26.** mL
12. 16 **27.** L
13. 3 **28.** 0.0505
14. 4 **29.** 406,200
15. by the pint **30.** 4

P. 37
1. divide **12.** 11
2. multiply **13.** 16
3. multiply **14.** 24
4. divide **15.** 16
5. divide **16.** 5
6. multiply **17.** 2 1/4
7. 6 **18.** 40
8. 48 **19.** 12
9. 14 **20.** 2
10. 32 **21.** 9
11. 12 **22.** 40 glasses

P. 38
1. Cheese Bake:
2 2/3 c flour
4 tsp baking powder
1 1/3 tsp salt
5 1/3 tsp butter
1 1/3 c grated cheddar cheese
8/9 c cold water

Potato Delight:
7 c bread crumbs
14 eggs
49 oz evaporated milk
3 1/2 tsp onion powder
10 1/2 tsp salt
5 1/4 tbsp Worcestershire sauce
14 potatoes
28 oz frozen vegetables
17 1/2 raw carrots
24 1/2 oz gravy

Pp. 39–40
1. 6 3/4 cups
2. 1.25 liters
3. 3,430 mL or 3.430 L
4. 1 1/2 cups
5. 3/4 pint
6. 4.7 liters
7. 15 dozen cookies
8. 48 days
9. 89.6 loads
10. more
11. 2.1 L
12. 33 minutes
13. 120 mL
14. 2,532 gallons
15. 6 quarts
16. 2 gallons

P. 41 Answers will vary. Check students' work for correct computation.

P. 42 Answers will vary. Check students' data for reasonable results.

Pp. 43–44
1. C **7.** B
2. A **8.** C
3. C **9.** B
4. C **10.** A
5. A **11.** C
6. B **12.** B

Pp. 45–46
1. 37° F **4.** 95° F
2. 53° F **5.** 12° F
3. 42° F **6.** 19° F
7-12. Check students' work.
13. 3° C **16.** 18° C
14. 26° C **17.** 12° C
15. 36° C **18.** 52° C
19-24. Check students' work.

P. 47
1. Noon
2. 10 A.M. and 11 A.M.
3. about 9° F
4. between 8 A.M. and 9 A.M. Check tables for accuracy.

P. 48 Students will accurately mark temperatures on scales.
1. 15° C **4.** 15° C
2. 30° C **5.** -8° C
3. 25° C **6.** 0° C

P. 49
1. 1991 **5.** about 17° F
2. 70° F **6.** about 67° F
3. about 12° F **7.** 1991
4. 1991 **8.** 1991

P. 50
1. -5° C
2. Monday, Tuesday, and Friday
3. 213° F
4. Yes. It would be too warm for ice if the temperature were 10° C.
5. 68° F
6. 69° F

P. 51 Answers will vary. Check students' graphs for reasonable data.

P. 52 Answers will vary. Check students' work for reasonable data.

Pp. 53–54
Unit 5 Assessment

1. B
2. A
3. C
4. B
5. A
6. A
7. C
8. B
9. A
10. B
11. C
12. C

Pp. 55-56

1. lb
2. oz
3. lb
4. T
5. b
6. b
7. 1
8. 2
9. 6,000
10. 32,000
11. 1/4
12. 6
13. 4 1/2 x 16 – 12 = 6 oz
14. kg
15. mg
16. g
17. kg
18. a
19. b
20. 17 portions
21. 8 portions
22. 24 portions
23. 20 portions
24. 65 ÷ 3 x 36 = 780 g

P. 57 Possible answers:

Left side	Scale reading	Right side
1 g	7 g	8 g
8 g	8 g	16 g
4 g	12 g	16 g
16 g	4 g	4 g + 16 g
4 g + 4 g	0	8 g
8 g	3 g	1 g + 4 g
8 g +16 g	19 g	1 g + 4 g
4 g + 8 g + 16 g	27 g	1 g
4 g + 8 g	5 g	16 g + 1 g
16 g + 4 g	7 g	1 g+ 4 g + 8 g
16 g	13 g	1g+4g+8g+16g
16 g + 4 g	11 g	1 g + 8 g
1 g + 4 g + 16 g	13 g	8 g
16 g	11 g	1 g + 4 g
28 g	1 g	1g+4g+8g+16g

P. 58

1. 550 pounds
2. Marble Creek
3. Marble Creek
4. Pine Ridge
5. Week 4
6. Pine Ridge: 500 pounds; Marble Creek: 450 pounds

P. 59

1. 26.9 pounds
2. 13.35 more pounds
3. 124 grams
4. 2 pounds, 13 ounces
5. 3 3/4 T
6. 12 more ounces
7. 1/4 kg
8. 3/4 pound

P. 60 Answers will vary. Check students' work for reasonable answers.

Pp. 61–62
Unit 6 Assessment

1. B
2. C
3. B
4. A
5. A
6. B
7. C
8. B
9. C
10. A

P. 63

1. 6:40 A.M.
2. 11:38 A.M.
3. 6:17 P.M.
4. Friday, 3:41 A.M.
5. 2 hr 28 min
6. 10 min 16 sec
7. 3 min 33 sec
8. 9 hr 3 min
9. 44 sec
10. 3 hr 26 min
11. 1 hr 55 min

P. 64

1. 48
2. 168
3. 9
4. 600
5. 21
6. 730
7. 3
8. 360
9. 13
10. 8, 18
11. 202
12. 7, 47
13. 1, 146
14. 5, 2
15. 17, 4
16. 17,520
17. 1, 48
18. 4
19. 604,800
20. 180 x 3 = 540 hours

P. 65

1. 9:40 A.M
2. 12:45 P.M.
3. 1:00 P.M.; 3:00 P.M.
4. It will arrive at 11:30 A.M. the following day.
5. 8:55 A.M.
6. Yes. There is a 1-hour wait between the plane's landing in Sarasota and the bus's departure.

P. 66

Name	Time
Annie	10:00 P.M.
Jamal	9:40 P.M.
Li	10:20 P.M.
David	11:05 P.M.
Enid	10:15 P.M.
Fred	10:35 P.M.
Jorge	11:35 P.M.

Name	Time
Annie	6:25 A.M.
Jamal	6:05 A.M.
Li	7:05 A.M.
David	7:00 A.M.
Enid	7:05 A.M.
Fred	7:30 A.M.
Jorge	8:30 A.M.

3. no one
4. David
5. David
6. Fred and Jorge
7. Enid
8. Fred and Jorge

P. 67

1. central
2. Pacific
3. 11:00 A.M.
4. eastern and central
5. 3 times
6. mountain

P. 68

1. 5 hours
2. 10 1/4 hours
3. 1/4 hour
4. 5 hours, 15 minutes
5. about 7 school days
6. 2 hours
7. 5 1/4 days
8. 3 hours

P. 69 Answers will vary. Check students' work for reasonable data.

P. 70 Answers will vary. Check students' work for reasonable data.

Pp. 71–72
Unit 7 Assessment

1. B
2. A
3. B
4. C
5. A
6. B
7. C
8. C
9. B
10. B
11. B
12. C

P. 73

1. three dollars and sixty cents; $3.60
2. two dollars and twenty-eight cents; $2.28
3. two dollars and eighty-two cents; $2.82
4. five dollars and thirty-seven cents; $5.37
5. four dollars and fifty-five cents; $4.55

P. 74

1. 8 nickels, 4 dimes, 2 quarters
2. 39 dimes, 60 pennies
3. 36 cents
4. 10 coins: 1 half-dollar, 1 quarter, 4 dimes, 4 pennies
5. 2 quarters, 10 nickels, 20 dimes
6. 4 quarters, 4 dimes, 12 nickels
7. 32 nickels, 10 pennies, 8 dimes

P. 75

1. yes; 7,411.5 pesetas = $45; 182.5 riyal = $50
2. 3,955.5 drachmas

Country	Mexico	Saudi Arabia	Egypt
Foreign currency	18,150 pesos	255.5 riyal	67.6 pounds
U.S. dollars	$55	$70	$52

Country	Greece	Spain	Norway
Foreign currency	9,097.65 drachma	625.86 pesetas	519.12 krone
U.S. dollars	$69	$3.80	$63

Pp. 76–77

1. 2 batteries, $0.22 left
2. Purity; Each package costs $2.09 at Supreme's.
3. $374.00
4. $300.00
5. $0.11, $2.31
6. $12.50 each
7. $8.00
8. $147.56
9. $16.90
10. $2.00 each
11. $0.30
12. $11,520.00

P. 78 Monitor partners as they guess and check.

P. 79 Answers will vary. Check students' work for reasonable data.

P. 80 Answers will vary. Check students' work for reasonable data.

Pp. 81–82
Unit 8 Assessment

1. B
2. C
3. A
4. A
5. B
6. C
7. A
8. C
9. B
10. C
11. B
12. A

P. 83

1. 24 m
2. 24 mm
3. 28 m
4. 57 ft
5. 40 cm
6. 22 ft
7. 50 m
8. 36 ft
9. 7 in.
10. 30 yd
11. 7 ft
12. 60 in.

P. 84

1. 70.0 mm
2. 48.7 mm
3. 56.2 mm
4. 89.5 mm
5. 26.9 cm
6. 8.2 cm
7. 60.4 cm
8. 42.7 cm
9. 75.0 cm

P. 85

1. 108 cm^2
2. 176 cm^2
3. 36 $in.^2$
4. 51 m^2
5. 78 $in.^2$
6. 720 mm^2
7. 900 mm^2
8. 110 mm^2

P. 86

1. 112 yd^2
2. 252 cm^2
3. 80 m^2
4. 160 ft^2
5. 28 mm^2
6. 18 mm^2

P. 87

1. 6 cm^2
2. 8 cm^2
3. 8 mi^2
4. 18 m^2
5. 4 cm^2
6. 63 in^2
7. 48 m^2
8. 85 ft^2
9. 14 ft^2
10. 21 ft^2
11. 36 in^2

P. 88

1. 3
2. 4
3. 12 m^2
4. 48 m^2
5. 24 m^2
6. study
7. 8 rolls
8. 54 m^2
9. 9 rolls

P. 89

1. 18 cubes
2. 27 cubes
3. 14 cubes
4. 24 cubes
5. 18 cubes
6. 12 cubes
7. 14 cubes
8. figure 4
9. figure 3, 5, and 6
10. about 30 blocks, no

P. 90

1. 63 cm^3
2. 72 cm^3
3. 40 cm^3
4. 72 cm^3
5. 60 cm^3
6. 64 cm^3
7. 15,000 ft^3
8. 882 $in.^3$
9. 280 $in.^3$
10. 1,000 ft^3
11. 12,500 yd^3

P. 91

1. 40 ft^2
2. 94.2 inches
3. 2,400 $inches^3$
4. 23 cm^2
5. 300 ft^2, 70 ft
6. 20 trees

P. 92 Answers will vary. Check students' plans.

P. 93 Answers will vary. Check students' work.

P. 94 Answers will vary. Check students' plans.